Sock Hunting and Other Pursuits of the WORKING MOTHER

by
PAM RAVAN

Aglow Publications

A Ministry of Women's Aglow Fellowship, Int'l.
P.O. Box 1548
Lynnwood, WA 98046-1548
USA

Cover design by David Marty

Women's Aglow Fellowship, International is a non-denominational organization of Christian women. Our mission is to provide support, education, training and ministry opportunities to help women worldwide discover their true identity in Jesus Christ through the power of the Holy Spirit.

Aglow Publications is the publishing ministry of Women's Aglow Fellowship, International. Our publications are used to help women find a personal relationship with Jesus Christ, to enhance growth in their Christian experience, and help them recognize their roles and relationship according to scripture.

For more information about Women's Aglow Fellowship, please write to Women's Aglow Fellowship International, P.O. Box 1548, Lynnwood, WA 98046-1548, USA or call (206) 775-7282.

Unless otherwise noted, all scripture quotations in this publication are from the Holy Bible, New International Version. Copyright 1973, 1978, 1984, International Bible Society. Other versions are abbreviated as follows: KJV (King James Version), TLB (The Living Bible), NAS (New American Standard).

© Copyright 1991, Pam Ravan. Published by Aglow Publications, A Ministry of Women's Aglow Fellowship, Int'l., Lynnwood, Washington, USA. All rights reserved. Except for brief quotations for review purposes, no part of this book may be reproduced in any form or by any electronic or mechanical means without prior permission from the publisher. Printed in the United States of America.

ISBN 0-932305-89-X

Thank you from Aglow Publications

Publication expenses for this book were underwritten by
Ordinary Women of the Great Lakes Region
Aglow women from Indiana, Michigan,
New York, and Ohio

with special thanks to Central Indiana women

"... 'Not by might nor by power, but by My Spirit,'
says the Lord of hosts" (Zech. 4:6 NAS)

April 1991

To all the working mothers of this world

Acknowledgments

Thank you—

Mom and Dad, Linda, my sister, and Tim, my husband, for helping me with my children while I wrote.

Cathy, my neighbor, for the same reason.

Grandmother. You know why.

Granddad, for helping me with scripture references when I couldn't find them in a concordance. You just knew where they were.

Connie Ebert, a wonderful librarian who was of great assistance to me.

Authors and experts who so graciously granted permission for me to quote them.

Gloria Chisholm, my editor, for all the encouragement as I worked on this project.

Contents

Introduction		11
Chapter 1	Look Who's Working Now	13
Chapter 2	The Marketplace	23
Chapter 3	Trenches and Pits	33
Chapter 4	The Guilt Trip	43
Chapter 5	What's Realistic and What's Not?	53
Chapter 6	High Wires and Teeter-Totters	65
Chapter 7	Help! The Ravenous Multitude Is after Me	77
Chapter 8	The Sock Hunt	89
Chapter 9	Everyone Wants Something from Me...	101
Chapter 10	Is Love Possible on a Tight Schedule?	113
Source Notes		125
Support Groups—Places of Growth and Healing		131

Introduction

The 1990s bring us unprecedented change in every aspect of life. But nowhere are those changes more profound than in the area of mothering.

In the nineties, mothers will enter the work force in greater numbers than ever before. Cheryl Russell in *100 Predictions for the Baby Boom* estimates that eighty percent of mothers will work outside the home by 1995.[1]

While the number of working mothers has risen drastically and their life-styles changed accordingly, much of Christian literature for women is still written to the full-time homemaker. This creates a void for many women when they desperately need encouragement and insight.

Sock Hunting and Other Pursuits of the Working Mother is a support book for women who wonder: "How can I work and still have energy to nurture my family? How can I motivate my family (without nagging) to help with the daily chores? What is the best way to handle job/family conflicts?"

We will take a hard look at the guilt and expectations of the working mother. Much published material is available that addresses the working mother in a positive manner, providing helpful organizational tips. However, I sometimes feel fatigued just reading the things I should be doing to make life easier.

In this book, we will deal more with inner issues such as attitudes and priorities than with perfectly organized closets, drawers, or garages. We'll learn to live with those things that, try as we might, we can't get done.

1
...
Look Who's Working Now

Like many mothers who work, Susan feels stretched. She fed her kids oatmeal for breakfast this morning (some on the wall, some in their ears, and some in their mouths). One of the beds didn't get made, and the floors are a mess. Last night the sink plugged up—she had asked three-year-old Lacy to put the dirty socks into the washing machine, not the garbage disposal. Water spewed everywhere until she and her husband could get it turned off. They spent the rest of the evening fixing it, so she didn't bake a cake for her daughter to take to the school carnival.

Susan buckled Lacy into her car seat and when she and her son Petey were fastened, too, she started the car and backed out of the driveway.

"Mom, I got to go to the bathroom!" Petey cried. By the way he squirmed, Susan knew he meant it.

"Oh, Petey, I wish you'd said so sooner." Susan pulled

Sock Hunting and Other Pursuits

back into the driveway, and Petey raced into the house.

Susan looked at her watch every thirty seconds, wishing he'd hurry. Finally, he climbed back into the car. They sped to the babysitter's and dropped Lacy off. It began to rain and as Susan ran back to the car, big droplets soaked through her freshly pressed blouse. She started the car once again and headed toward the grade school.

As they rounded the corner, a line of cars in front of her slowed to a stop. Some possibly otherwise intelligent human being was trying to move a house in the middle of rush hour traffic. Cars quickly closed in behind her. Another ten minute wait. She really was going to be late for work.

Finally traffic inched forward in slow motion while her mind raced. Would she make it?

"Momma, when I went back into the house to go to the bathroom, I took my backpack and I left it there. It has my permission slip in it. Now I can't go to the pumpkin patch!"

School policy was "no permission slip, no field trip." Susan knows she will be late if she goes into the school to fill out another form. She also knows that if she doesn't go in, Petey won't be able to go, and he's looked forward to this trip for weeks.

Sound contrived? Maybe scenes like this are unfamiliar to you. If so, I'm happy for you. You don't need this book.

But for the rest of us . . .

How do we cope when we are unable to get it all done? Our coworkers come in early, stay late, take work home, and represent the company on their time off at everything from blood drives to the company softball team, while working moms cook, clean, tuck their children into bed, and drive car pools.

As working moms (referred to as WMs in this book), we have made domestic choices that leave us limited time for career development. Therefore, we don't often rise to the top of the corporate ladder, although this is changing as more companies are becoming "family friendly" to accommodate us. As we enter the '90s, more companies are exploring the possible advantages of flextime, job share alternatives to full-time employment. Many companies are also implementing on-site day-care options. Yet despite these changes, most WMs aren't working so they can ride in the company Lear Jet or eat lunch in Paris twice a week.

WHY DO MOTHERS WORK?

Kay Kuzma, associate professor of health sciences at Loma Linda University's School of Health, touched on this in her book *Working Mothers*. "As a result of many changes in our society during the last decade, the picture of a woman's role has begun to change."[1] She says that many couples today find it difficult to achieve economic stability on one income. "The fact is, women with children are working . . . more than half of all mothers in the country. Many of these mothers are single parents who must work. Others who have a choice have exercised it and chosen to work."[2]

According to statistics from the Bureau of Labor, sixty-eight percent of mothers between the ages of eighteen to fifty-five are WMs.[3]

These numbers have nearly doubled in the past twenty years. In the late 1960s only thirty-five percent of mothers participated in outside employment.[4]

As the statistics climbed, an alarm arose within circles that viewed women's participation in the marketplace as a threat to traditional values.

"Although the working father has been honored and upheld as an ideal parent, the working mother has long been cast in negative shadows."[5] The following from an

Sock Hunting and Other Pursuits

article written by Vicky Warren for *Christian Psychology For Today,* a magazine published by Mirnith-Meier Clinic of Dallas, Texas, poignantly describes some of these negative shadows.

> If anyone had told me when my son was born that three years later I would find myself back in the work force, I would have said, "Never!" I had designed my blueprint for motherhood—and it did not include returning to work! But, "The mind of man plans his way, but the Lord directs his steps" (Prov. 16:9). My carefully charted course through motherhood took an unexpected detour; and I did, indeed, find myself a working mom.
>
> The purpose of this article is not to debate the pros and cons of whether or not mothers should work but to offer encouragement to those who do. Work is a fact of life for many women today; and we, as Christians, need to get about the business of offering support and encouragement rather than heaping on guilt and condemnation.
>
> The Christian homemaker/mother is waging an uphill battle against societal attitudes that would rob her of the recognition and dignity that are deservedly hers. But, unfortunately, it seems that Christian mothers who work are now having to wage a similar battle—only this battle is from within the body of Christ. [*Work* is a word with four letters, but to many it is a "dirty word"] when used in the same sentence as "mother." Working moms are often made to feel as if they should be in a self-help group, making the confession, "My name is _____, and I'm a working mother."[6]

Look Who's Working Now

The impact of the above mentality began to hit home the day I attended a Sunday school class in a different church than the one we usually attended. We were discussing God's plan for the family when suddenly one of the men in the class began to "prophesy."

"The Devil is on the throne of your home!" he said in an authoritative voice. "You get up in the morning and spend too much time painting your face and combing your hair. Then you paint your nails. Your children get their own breakfast while you put on your outer adornments. You leave your home and go out into the world and work so you can have lunch with your girlfriends. . . . Meanwhile, the Devil is on the throne of your home."

I felt a little bit like the paintbrush my son Joel had tried to clean the previous week by sticking it (bristles first) into the electric pencil sharpener; it wasn't a pleasant experience, but it did provide some material for provocative thought.

A couple of letters printed in *Focus on the Family* magazine provide material for further thought. These excerpts depict the different ways women view each other and how they view outside employment.

The first excerpt is from a stay-at-home mother. She says (of WMs): "I think some of them work to avoid the responsibility of raising their children. Some days, I wouldn't mind getting dressed up, going off to work and having somebody else watch after the kids. But I know that wouldn't be best for them."[7]

The second excerpt comes from a working mom. She writes: "I notice a breach between the women who stay home with the children and the women who work. I don't want to see that. I really don't. It hurts. I feel it now. I would like to see that breach mended, but I don't know how to go about that."[8]

Sock Hunting and Other Pursuits

Any WM who has been asked pointed questions by well-meaning individuals about her motives for working would have an idea of how this woman feels.

We all laughed several years ago when Rodney Dangerfield paved his road to success as a comedian with his bewildered expression and famous one-liner, "I just can't get no respect." However, it wasn't until I became a working mother that his words became somewhat real to me. In touching upon WMs and their need for respect, Vicky Warren writes:

Hebrews 10:24, 25 speaks volumes to the need in this area. ". . . let us consider how to stimulate one another to love and good deeds . . . encouraging one another."

The message is frequently conveyed that working mothers have sacrificed the security and well-being of their children on the altar of their own egos and personal greed. Let's leave the job of judging motives where it belongs—with the Lord (Prov. 16:2). Let's busy ourselves with stimulating one another to love and good deeds.[9]

Perhaps we have mixed feelings about working mothers because we are treading new ground. "There is no historical track record that tells us what works and what doesn't. There's no road map with the potholes clearly marked. We are like inventors, trying out a new invention for the first time, with no data that tells us what to expect."[10]

However, there is help.

When Jesus called his first disciples, Simon, James, and John, he called them from their workplace, the shore of Lake Gennesaret. Fishermen, they had worked hard all night, but their efforts were seemingly wasted; they hadn't

Look Who's Working Now

caught anything. Tired and discouraged, they brought in their boat and began to wash their nets.

Meanwhile, Jesus spoke to a crowd by the water's edge. When the people began to press closer to him, he got into Simon's boat. He taught the people from the boat while Simon and James and John continued to clean their nets.

"When he finished speaking, he said to Simon, 'Put out into the deep water and let down the nets for a catch.'

"Simon answered, 'Master, we've worked hard all night and haven't caught anything. But because you say so, I will set down the nets.'

"When they had done so, they caught such a large number of fish that their nets began to break" (Luke 5:4-6).

Jesus took a non-judgmental interest in the professional lives of Simon, James, and John before ever calling them to be disciples. He assisted them without questioning their motives, although James and John, nicknamed "Sons of Thunder" due to their tempers, probably needed help. Simon made an appropriate partner for this wild duo. He's the one who, after being with Jesus for three years, cut off another man's ear because he didn't like what the man said and did.

Jesus didn't care about any of that. As far as we know, he didn't inquire about the reasons behind their decision to become fishermen, whether it was because they really needed the money or not. He didn't seem to care that two men would later fight with others over who would be the greatest, or get their mother to ask special favors for them. After all, they could have wanted to show their prowess as fishermen.

Jesus helped them even though they may have just wanted a big catch that day so they wouldn't have to work the next. In other words, they could have been avoiding responsibility.

Sock Hunting and Other Pursuits

These aspects may have mattered to others, but Jesus wasn't concerned. His only concern was to show these men *his* power and *his* plan for their lives.

Later he said, ". . . Don't be afraid; from now on you will catch men" (Luke 5:10).

In this book we'll neither question nor justify the motives of the working mother. Rather, we'll explore ways to help us do what we are already doing.

If somewhere along the line Jesus says, "Put down the nets," then so be it. But in the meantime, he is concerned with our professional lives. He wants to help us.

His word has given us a wonderful example of a working woman in Proverbs 31. Author Vicky Warren elaborates on this chapter:

> See how she managed to juggle the demands of home and work and yet is held up in Scripture as the "ideal" wife and mother. Here was a woman who apparently left many of her domestic duties to her "maidens" while she was involved in buying fields, planting vineyards from her earnings, making and selling linen garments and supplying belts to the tradesmen (vv. 16, 24). She may not have gone off to an office every day, but the nature of her work surely would have necessitated her being away quite a bit. And yet, Scripture tells us that "She looks well to the ways of her household and does not eat the bread of idleness. . . . Her children rise up and bless her; her husband also, and praises her . . . (vv. 26, 28).
>
> How do we do this without totally burning out? The essential ingredient is stewardship—developing the ability to prioritize in three crucial areas: redeeming the time, refining your talents, and recognizing your treasures.[11]

The following prayer, written by Jody Detrick, addresses these areas.

> Unclutter me, Lord, Take a strong hand to the disarray of jumbled thought and activities in my life. They pile one upon another like years worth of junk compressed into a small closet, just waiting to tumble down on an unwary victim who chances to open the door. I want to be cleaned out. I sense the need for space, extra room in my affections, room for growing a more deeply committed love.
>
> I sense the need for free time, unscheduled stretches of time when I can sit at Your feet without watching the clock.
>
> I am a gatherer, Lord. I tend to pick up so many projects, so many plans, goals, and ideas that require serious effort. I generally gather good things, Father, but in quantity that doesn't allow for any to develop into best.
>
> Please help me to narrow my output of energy into the channels best suited for bringing You the maximum glory from my life. I would rather be one mighty, rushing river than many diverted, weak streams.
>
> Keep reminding me that I am not omnipotent. I cannot do everything myself. Nor can I try to be everyone else without failing to be myself.
>
> Above all, give me the wisdom to know which of those good things to allow to pass, and which to hold onto and pursue with all I have until it becomes my best to you.[12]

TIME TO CONSIDER

1. How do you deal with the feelings of frustration that come as a result of being overwhelmed in your dual role

Sock Hunting and Other Pursuits

as working mother? How do you maintain your inner peace and composure in the rush of work commitments and the TLC needed at home?

2. How have you arrived at your personal convictions about being a mother in the work force? What goals do you hope to accomplish as a wage earner?

3. Ruth was a working woman. What did Boaz tell those who might otherwise have made discouraging remarks to her (Ruth 2:11-17)?

4. How do you feel when negative attitudes about working mothers are directed toward you personally? How can you mend the breach between stay-at-home mothers and working mothers?

2

The Marketplace

Although the number of mothers in the work force doubled since the early sixties, the *role* of WMs in the marketplace has held steady. The majority of working moms are classified as blue-collar with secretarial and sales jobs. Only five percent are managers or executives.[1]

Perhaps these figures represent the full circle that secular literature has come in the last two-and-a-half decades. We read the early, strong feminist message of Gloria Steinem, the modifications in Betty Friedan's *Second Look* ten years later, and finally the form of traditionalism in Arlene Rossen Cardozo's *Sequencing*. All defined *mother*.

The early feminist movement depicted motherhood as "a condition of terminal psychological and social decay, total self-abnegation and physical deterioration."[2]

Then in 1981, feminists denounced some of their earlier, more militant messages, and Betty Friedan wrote (referring

Sock Hunting and Other Pursuits

to reactionary effects of the feminist movement), "Some women remain imprisoned by that reaction, merely shifting their focus from . . . family to . . . career, exchanging one half-life for another . . . denying real aspects of herself and satisfactions of life. . . ."[3]

Let's look at one woman, Carla, and her response to work and family.

CARLA

Carla, though her career is on track, wonders if she's missing something. A thirty-nine-year-old computer software salesperson recently promoted to division manager, she has worked all her adult life for a job like this.

She now has the big plush office, the nearly limitless expense account, and the opportunity to travel often enough to rack up frequent flyer miles to Tahiti every six months. She has always dreamed of this. Yet she feels empty—even used—when she thinks of what she went through to get here.

Her two small children (whom she rarely sees before the hired nanny they call "Mommy" puts them to bed at night) spend every weekend with her ex-husband who, when they were married, complained that she didn't have time for anything but her job.

Now that she "has it all" she's not sure what "it" is. When she looks in the mirror, she sees a tired woman in a stiff business suit with empty eyes, surrounded by perfect makeup, perfect hair, perfect fingernails, and hands that haven't tied a little person's shoes in months.

But, she reminds herself, this person has a big desk, an expense account, frequent traveler miles—and tears rolling down her cheeks.

While many women remain on the "fast track," Arlene Rossen Cardozo observed in her book *Sequencing* yet another view of motherhood.

The Marketplace

Superwoman, the 120-hour-a-week dual-lifer who worked full-time at a high-powered career while trying to raise her children nights and weekends, is dead....

Instead, an increasing number of educated, career-experienced women are taking control of their adult lives by sequencing them into three stages: stage one, the full-time career; stage two, full-time mothering; and stage three, reincorporating a career in new ways so that family and profession complement rather than conflict."[4]

Now that the secular media *has* come full circle, even occasionally encouraging mothers to stay home with their children, inflation has added financial pressure. Some families need two incomes to pay for basics. This could be one reason that sixty-eight percent of mothers remain employed outside the home.[5]

However, keeping in mind the changing definitions of *mother* in the past two-and-a-half decades, it's a wonder that her *role* in the work-a-day world has remained fairly consistent. More mothers work, but they perform the same types of blue-collar jobs as they did twenty-five years ago.

Why is this? Rather than assume that working mothers are not gifted in the work force, or that they can't quite pull it together to ensure a worthwhile career, the statistics could represent something else. Perhaps women with the responsibilities and joys of raising children have recognized the time and effort involved in such an undertaking. Perhaps they have chosen lower ranking titles with less responsibilities, freeing more time and energy for family. These women may have valued home life over higher economic and social positions. But why? Could statistics represent the dedication that working mothers feel to their families?

Sock Hunting and Other Pursuits

Mothers are now defining what is important to them. The statistics could indicate a devotion to family that has withstood the age of "yuppiedom." If so, WMs are to be applauded, not criticized, for their choices. Although traditional values are under attack, they may yet remain intact in the hearts of mothers.

What about those who *do* occupy positions of prestige? Have these women "sold out" their families for their careers? Or, as I heard one woman put it, have "they, like Esau, given up their birthright to nurture their families for a mess of corporate porridge"?

Although I'll not presume to judge another, I will point out that lower paying positions aren't *always* the best for a WM's job satisfaction and family compatibility. In fact, they can sometimes be a detriment. Many of these jobs come not only with the disadvantage of lower pay but oftentimes include little control over working hours and conditions. These factors can diminish job/family satisfaction. Such was true for Candy.

CANDY

The employment advertisement promised a relaxed atmosphere in a small legal office. Although her new boss possessed all the charm of a true sanguine, after only a short time on the job, Candy began to wonder if he was trained in office etiquette by Morton Downey, Jr. or Saddam Hussein. He left the office for his usual three-hour lunches before giving her needed data to complete documents he wanted delivered the next morning. When he returned at 3:30 P.M. she would *then* be presented with information to complete the papers.

She arrived home late more often than not and spent many evenings and weekends doing work she could have completed at the office if her boss had provided her with

The Marketplace

the needed data.

Eventually, Candy accepted another position as office manager in a large legal firm. This new position required less overtime, and she had more control over when and how long. For Candy, a higher profile, higher paying job worked to her and her family's advantage.

For many single moms, an elevated position with higher pay may be not only desirable but necessary to support a family. Janie is such a mom.

JANIE

Janie, a single mom, worked two jobs to keep her family financially afloat—until she was offered a managerial position with an accounting firm. For her, a step up the ladder has made the difference between working one job instead of two to provide for her children.

What about women who are entering traditionally male-dominated fields such as construction? Are they smothering their femininity by trying to be men? I think now of Lynette.

LYNETTE

Lynette, mother of two boys, is a finish worker for a construction company. Before going into construction, she operated a day-care and later combined a series of odd jobs: bookkeeping from her home, house-cleaning two days a week, and a small crafts business.

It came about when a man from her church asked if she wanted to do finish work on some apartments he was building. He told her that if she started early she could be home by 3:00 P.M. (when her boys came home from school), and she could make as much in two days as she had in a week with all of her odd jobs combined. She quickly said yes.

Sock Hunting and Other Pursuits

For the first time since her husband left, they had money for something besides bills. For her, construction work has been good.

Whatever a mother's role in the workplace, if it's an honest means of employment, it's to be respected. For a mother to work is a stretching experience requiring a nearly indefatigable effort (whatever the occupation). The last thing she needs is to become involved in what *Special Report* termed as the "Mommy Wars."

WHAT'S A "MOMMY WAR"?

Special Report: Family defines a mommy war as "moms slinging verbal stones at other moms who have made work-and-family decisions that differ from theirs."

What facilitated such a war?

What happened was this: In the past 10 years, more moms have spent days in the workplace than at home. This increase in two-paycheck households has refocused attention on the work-and-family juggling act. (Add everyone's heartfelt desire to do the right thing for the children and the tendency to pass judgement on folks who aren't doing things *our* way) and you have a volatile atmosphere.[6]

Another article on mommy wars said:

It also comes from the "we want everyone to share our method, since it's made us so happy" syndrome. We firmly believe that we've found the one true way, and everyone else should know it. . . . If they're not doing the same thing we do, it's simply because they haven't heard about it. So we tell them. Again and again.

The Marketplace

If you suspect that other people are doing something different in the parenting arena, it raises a possibility, not that they could be right, too, but that you might be wrong. And you so dearly wish to be right that you get defensive....[7]

What can we learn from the various ways we approach motherhood? If nothing else, we can learn to respect one another, to resist lashing out and in defense stamping a "poor quality" label on those who approach work and mothering differently than we do.

After all, what do we know? I am reminded of Paul's words: "So be careful not to jump to conclusions before the Lord returns as to whether someone is a good servant [mother] or not. When the Lord comes, he will turn on the light so that everyone can see exactly what each one of us is really like deep down in our hearts." He goes on to explain that *then* everyone will know why we have been doing the work we've been doing. "At that time, each will receive his praise from God."[8]

No one has discovered the perfect way to mother—yet. We have our beliefs and do our best to carry them out. However, sometimes we fall short. We miss a family member's need. We forget something important. While we try to keep these times to a minimum, they still happen. We are mothers. *Human* mothers. The best we can do for our children is to be gracious to ourselves—not excusing our failures, but acknowledging them to ourselves and to our children. By doing this, we impart to them the wisdom of love and tolerance, not only for ourselves, but toward others.

Our children's sense of security comes, not from the fact that we work or do not work, not from whether we work blue-collar or carry a briefcase, but from our

Sock Hunting and Other Pursuits

assurance that the life we live with them is the life we *want* to live.

Doctors Robert Hemfelt, Frank Minirth, and Paul Meier spoke of this assurance in their book *We Are Driven* when they wrote: "Children have a comfortable sense of pride and security when they know that their parents like themselves just as they are. Growing up with a dad [mom] who drives off whistling every day to his [her] job as a janitor is healthier than watching a dad [mom] agonize over an executive position he [she] hates."[9]

Our responsibility as mothers is neither to stay home or go to work. It's to portray this sense of security to our children. We do this by changing what we can change and deciding to be joyful amidst the rest.

God hasn't left us on our own in this area. He promised he would give us joy in whatever our circumstances. There are a lot of dead-end jobs out there and WMs fill many of these positions. Sometimes these jobs feel like a prison with all the "freedom" they allot to us.

But for now, remember the story of Paul and Silas in prison. Certainly, they weren't too pleased with their physical surroundings. Slimy water lined the prison walls. Lack of sanitary facilities caused a stench that nearly choked the breath out of them, and it was unbearably cold at night. Besides all of that, Paul was an extremely talented and educated man. He was well aware that his gifts and abilities far exceeded anything he might accomplish in a dark, drab hole, singing songs to an audience of criminals.

As WMs we, too, sometimes end up in jobs with little reward. We feel frustrated. But if we take our frustration home every night, out children are the beneficiaries.

Whenever parents are unhappy with themselves or don't have a clear vision of who they are, an air of

The Marketplace

uncertainty and shame permeates the home. Children grow up unsure of what to expect next. They know only that Mom and Dad don't like the way things are. The status quo must be bad, the kids surmise, and therefore it becomes a source of shame.[10]

In their prison experience, Paul and Silas sang praises in the midst of *criminals*, and the earth beneath them began to shake and the prison doors flew open. Our *children* make a much better audience for our praise than the criminals did. Besides that, joy and thankfulness will encourage us personally and professionally far better than frustration and despair.

While we can take many physical steps to give our best to our job and to our families, the most important step is attitudinal.

As WMs, we have more than enough to keep us occupied. To perform so many varied tasks each day and to do each one in love is a challenge, and although we do our best, sometimes we fail. The following poem by Catherine Mercier illustrates what we can offer our kids whether we succeed or fail:

> I am a mother, only human
> I do not always know what to do
> Sometimes I'm much too busy
> Sometimes I yell at you.
> But all my love
> I give you for strength, stand tall and sure in this life.
> All my pride
> I give you for confidence and the courage
> to do what is right.
> Compassion
> I give you for gentleness, help others

Sock Hunting and Other Pursuits

as you've been helped at home.
The Word of God
I teach you, so you'll never be alone.
No kids, I am not perfect,
nor rich, nor strong, nor wise.
But my darlings, if you take these gifts
You'll have rich and wonderful lives.[10]

TIME TO CONSIDER

1. What outstanding quality is mentioned in Proverbs 3:17? Why is this noteworthy?

2. How does God say we are to approach our work (Col. 3:23)? How can you practically and specifically apply this in your job?

3. How can Hebrews 10:24 help us in our jobs? How does this relate to working with those who aren't Christians?

4. Why did Paul say what he did in Galatians 6:4? In what ways will you benefit by following these instructions? How will those around you benefit by your following these instructions?

3

Trenches and Pits

Dodie-Do-It-All frantically piles the last breakfast dish into an already overloaded dishwasher. "Why didn't someone run this thing last night?" she mutters. "It's only 8:30 A.M., and I'm already off schedule." It's Saturday, but she nevertheless has work to do.

Dodie's to do list reads like the books of Numbers and Chronicles, tedious and repetitive, stretching into the wee hours of the next morning. Dodie assures herself, "If I just try hard enough, I'm sure I can get this all done." She glances over her list:

7:45-8:45 A.M.	Breakfast, dishes, and devotions
9:00-10:50	Help at school
11:00-11:45	Grocery shop
11:45-12:00	Put food away
12:00-2:00 P.M.	Sew uniform for Susie
2:00-4:00	Clean house

Sock Hunting and Other Pursuits

4:00-5:30	Make dinner for company
6:00-9:00	Eat, clean up, and entertain guests
9:00-11:30	Bake cookies, cake, and bread for church sale
12:00-1:00 A.M.	Finish handcrafted present for cousin.

Dodie's motto: "A mom can get a lot done if she schedules herself." She sits down and begins to read her favorite devotional book, *How to Touch the Heart of God in 20 Seconds*. The phone rings.

"I wish someone would put out a devotional that doesn't take so long to get through," she mutters as she picks up the phone.

"What did you say?" her friend Wendy-Workaholic pants breathlessly into the other end of the line.

"Ugh . . . I just meant to say 'Hello.' "

"Well, no matter, I called to tell you that Janie is sick. I told Hillary that you'd take Janie's place and help us at the hospital auxiliary fund-raiser tomorrow night. We need you at the booth from 7:00 to 11:00 P.M."

Dodie would love to tell Wendy-Workaholic no, but Wendy works ten more hours a week than Dodie does, yet Wendy still manages to do all the little extras. Dodie had planned to use tomorrow night to catch up on tonight's missed sleep, yet she finds herself saying, "Okay, I'll be there."

As she sits down to finish her reading, the phone rings again. It's her boss.

"Dodie, Linda has an illness in the family. Will you take her 3:00 to 7:00 P.M. shift tomorrow? We really need you."

Even though she knows she'll be working her own shift during the day and the fund-raiser in the evening, that she'll go to work with little (if any) sleep, Dodie-Do-It-

Trenches and Pits

All says, "Sure, I'll be there." After all, she said the magic words—"We need you."

Dodie pushes thoughts of fatigue aside. She quotes, "I can do all things through Christ, who strengthens me," and resumes her hurried reading: "Every expenditure of energy ought to yield bread for the soul."[1]

Dodie decides this "spiritual" statement was written by a man who had nothing to do all day but write "spiritual" statements. Yes, she's certain this man never cleaned a kitchen floor while an army of neighborhood boys trailed his son to the refrigerator 430 times a day. Nor has he dealt with upset coworkers or a crabby boss all day. His car never quit on the freeway as he drove home from work. And he probably didn't arrive home and pick dog hairs out of his favorite sweater. She doubts that *his* kids let the dog into *his* room, and *his* dog probably didn't curl up on *his* fresh dry cleaning that waited to be put away.

Then she notices that he goes on to say: "In all my experiences . . . the soul should find its nutriment. Nothing should be spiritually empty."[2]

Humph. He must have been deprived of some of the more trying situations in life, she reasons. She doubts *his* son would invite the neighbor boy over to ride his skateboard down the stairs of the deck with him. *He* probably never had to explain to the neighbors why his boy's arm hung at a funny angle. No wonder he would write this stuff.

"Let me not pile up money and starve my soul."[3]

"It's time to get real," Dodie grunts. How many working moms worry about piling up too much money? After all, the violin rental, the gymnastic lessons, the soccer uniform, and the dental bill have ways of keeping a working mom's pile at a manageable level.

However, as she considers the last part of the above

Sock Hunting and Other Pursuits

writer's request, she has to admit that, as working moms, we probably don't hoard large sums of money, but amidst the hustle to get the family out the door, get ourselves to work on time, come home, feed the family, and put our homes in some semblance of order, time pressures provide the perfect opportunity for soul deprivation.

But what does that mean?

THE STARVED SOUL

A starved soul is one that is driven by frenzied activity, so much so that the warmth and joy of living evade it.

A starved soul keeps moving although it's dying inside. A starved soul aches for warmth and gentleness and love yet rarely takes time for a hug.

A starved soul's frustration mounts until thought patterns focus only on the irritations. A starved soul is empty, yet it takes no time to do the things that would nourish it.

A starved soul has no mercy on itself and therefore finds it hard to be tolerant of others. A starved soul longs to be kind yet lacks the energy to reach out.

As working mothers, we enter the working trenches either out of necessity or by choice. We do it because we believe we are capable of doing it. We do it because we believe we'll benefit. Some of us have the support of our families. Others of us have found ourselves either physically and/or emotionally alone, working a job that in prior years wasn't attempted even in two-parent households.

In such a climate the precarious balance between work and home can tip, toppling us into a pit instead of the mere trench we'd bargained for.

Included in the list of trenches and pits are mistakes we make *before* we are hired. In fact, some mistakes occur even before the interview takes place. These oversights often interfere with job satisfaction and family relations.

JOB SEARCH GONE SOUR

Many women approach a job search after having children the same way they approached it before they had a family. You may ask, "What's wrong with that? It worked before; it should work now."

It *will* work. It will get you a job. However, it may not be the *right* job, the one you will be happy with or the one that fits your family's needs.

Why is this?

We can become so intent on "getting" a job that we don't carefully think through our needs and what we have to offer. Knowing these things *before* seeking employment possibilities is essential.

Before we had families, it was easy to answer an ad in the newspaper and simply adjust to whatever the job required. Now, however, children aren't always able to understand, let alone cope, with our life-style changes. We must take their needs and coping capabilities into consideration. In doing so, the price of that adjustment may be too high a price to pay.

As moms, we need to know certain things about our places of employment. Will we be on-call twenty-four hours a day, or will the company allow us to care for a sick child? Does the employer view working moms as valuable to the company even though they may be only part-time, or occasionally want to attend a school function? Will it be difficult for our child to call us at work? Some employers understand these occasional requirements; others look upon them as intrusions. In all fairness to employers, some occupations and businesses lend themselves better to these unexpected happenings.

It takes time and research to find a job that fits your family's needs as well as your own. Take your time.

Sock Hunting and Other Pursuits

While no job is perfect (always allow for give and take), some positions are better suited to what you and your family need.

RUNAWAY EMOTIONS AND MOTHER/CHILD SEPARATIONS

In a recent interview with Patricia Rushford, pediatric counselor and author of *What Kids Need Most in a Mom,* I asked, *"Do you see common pitfalls for women as they reenter the job market after having children?"*

Rushford: I think one of the most common yet least explored challenges of working mothers is the sense of emotional loss and suffering that may come with the working separation between mother and child. We hear a lot about the effects this separation has on the child, but emotionally, the mother may have a strong reaction as well.

What type of a reaction?

Rushford: A woman may feel a sense of grief or sadness as she drops her child off at the babysitter. She may also feel a sense of loss. Their life together is changing. She will no longer be the one to get him up from his nap or feed him lunch. I remember feeling jealous of my mother-in-law because she spent so much time with my child.

What advice do you have to offer?

Rushford: First, recognize that, as with any change in life, becoming a working mom has an emotional impact on the entire family. Give yourself the opportunity to be sad if you feel sad. If a mother squelches these feelings, she only intensifies them. Part of the problem may be the unexpected quality to these feelings. She thought she wanted to go back to work but may not have realized that she would feel like this or that her family would also react to a sense of loss. She may not have thought these feelings through ahead of time and may actually feel guilty because she has them. The guilt can convince her that there is something wrong with her when, in fact, these feelings are quite normal.

What can a mother do to help herself and her family work through some of these emotions?

Rushford: How she deals with these feelings of loss will affect the way her children cope with them. A great deal can be accomplished if she discusses them with her children in an intelligent and positive manner.

What do you mean by a "positive manner"?

Rushford: If your child knows you feel guilty about something, that child will play it back to you. For instance, if you approach the mother/child separation with an "Oh, it's so hard. I hate leaving you; I feel so bad," attitude, then the child will play that attitude back to you. However, if a mother is understanding, yet reassuring, as in "You know, sometimes it's hard, but we'll be together again tonight," the child plays off of her like a mirror. If she is comfortable and happy, her child is more likely to be comfortable and happy.[4]

UNDERVALUING YOUR ABILITIES

Many mothers (especially those absent from the job market for a while or without formal education) may undervalue their worth and what they can contribute to a company.

Take Debbie, for instance. When the woman in personnel called to inform Debbie that the community college where she'd applied for a job wanted to hire her, she said, "The position starts at X dollars a month." Debbie accepted. Not until after details had been worked out and her contract signed did Debbie discover her position was covered by a grant—a grant prepared to pay several hundred dollars more each month.

Sock Hunting and Other Pursuits

"The time for salary negotiation is *before* you are hired," Debbie now says. "It would take years to make up that money in raises. Over a twenty-four-month period, which is how long I kept the position, it would have added up to seven thousand dollars. I should have asked, 'I understand you are offering X dollars. Is there any flexibility to that?'"

Although being underpaid probably won't deprive a working mom's soul, it can be an irritant that may be avoided simply by awareness of your skills and their worth in the marketplace. Remember, "A laborer is worthy of his wages."[5]

THE NURTURE TRAP

Mothers are conditioned to nurture. While this is a wonderful, loving quality, beware! In the job market it can backfire.

The ability to meet needs is normally an asset, but a mother may find an employer who needs her skills, and she may accept a job without realizing it doesn't fit *her* needs. She agrees to the responsibility out of her habit pattern: "Here is a need; I have the ability to fulfill it." While she may enjoy the feeling of competence at first, unless this position meets *some* of her own needs or unless she is Joan of Arc's sister, she will eventually become frustrated.

> We have chosen to be working mothers, but we have not yet been able to shed the old expectations. We still hope, secretly, to be both working mothers and traditional mothers. Simple physics should make it clear that such a combination is unworkable, but still we try. We shield our children from our working in feeble attempts to resemble, as best we can, our own at-home mothers. Because we often feel guilty about

working, we tend not to talk about it as often as we might, or in as positive terms as we might. There is sometimes a furtive quality about our lives, which inhibits us from making it clear in the workplace that we are working mothers who have responsibilities at home, or from making it clear at home that we are workers with responsibilities elsewhere.[5]

SLAVES TO OUR FREEDOM

We either become workaholics or working drudges. After all, the components are there. For a mother to try to work full-time *and* keep her home the way Momma did simply isn't realistic. Most of our stay-at-home moms put all of their energies into their homes. To expect the same smooth-running house, quantity and quality time with our families, plus give a job our all is unreasonable. That's only possible somewhere in Fantasy Land or on the road that exhausted, gasping workaholics race down to see who can go crazy first.

"Workaholism and the mothering of young children do not a happy combination make."[6] At least one three-year-old girl would agree with that statement. She said she wanted to grow up and be a father because "mommies work too hard."[7]

Perhaps Dodie-Do-It-All's devotional wasn't so silly after all:

Every expenditure of energy ought to yield bread for the soul. In all my experiences, be they grave or gay, the soul should find its nutriment. Nothing should be spiritually empty. Even my laughter should nourish my spirit.

O Lord my God, I pray that I may not toil for naught. *Let me not pile up money and starve my soul.*

Sock Hunting and Other Pursuits

Let me not seek after pleasures which provide no enduring joy. Let me so live toward Thee as to find the sacramental bread in every common thing. Lord, evermore give me this bread! For the sake of Christ Jesus. Amen.[8]

TIME TO CONSIDER

1. According to Ecclesiastes 3:1-8, what place should work take in our lives?

2. When do you feel most inadequate? How can you get beyond those feelings (Isa. 50:7; Ps. 55:22; Prov. 3:5, 6)?

3. What does the last part of Matthew 10:16 tell us we are to be in our dealings with the world? How can we apply this as working mothers? Can you think of any situations you are facing where this advice would be helpful?

4. What assurances can we have that God *wants* to help us (Ps. 32:8; 91:1, 2; James 1:5)? How can we help our children receive his assurance?

5. How can putting the scriptures mentioned above into practice assist us when we encounter pits and trenches?

4

The Guilt Trip

What is guilt, anyway?

One theory maintains we all need to say good-bye to guilt. Another says we must learn to live with it.

One dictionary says guilt is the fact or state of having done wrong; being to blame. Guilt can range from the vague nagging in one's brain that says, "You must pay your overdue library fines," to the debilitating mentality that says, "You're a loser; you can't do anything right; your life is a mess."

In the case of the library fines, simply paying the money we owe should eliminate the guilt—unless the mind continues to accuse us, "If you wouldn't have had those fines, you could have sent the money to starving children in the Romanian orphanages."

Even this kind of guilt isn't all bad. If it motivates us to return our books to the library on time so that we can use

Sock Hunting and Other Pursuits

the extra change more wisely, guilt will have served its purpose.

However, when guilt is tucked away, stuffed into our own special "guilt compressor," someday, someone may come along, push the right button, and our guilt may spew onto others our own pent-up shame.

I've asked hundreds of moms, "As a working mother, what, if anything, do you feel guilty about?" Following are some of their answers.

Jana (nurse and mother of three): "Sometimes I feel guilty about the time I spend away from my kids. I think I'm the best one to teach them and look out for them. I worry that fatigue and stress keeps me from perceiving my children's needs."

Elenore (factory worker and mother of one): "Not being able to attend school functions is one of the hardest things for me as a working mom. Most days, I leave before my daughter wakes in the morning. My husband feeds and dresses her. I wish I could be there for her like he is."

Margie (high school teacher and mother of two): "Not being able to stay home when one of the kids gets sick is difficult for me. And with small children under age five, it seems like they're continually sick from October to May.

"I also feel guilty about not performing at my best because of sleepless nights, running to doctor's appointments, racing home to attend to the kids, and putting non-priority work aside.

"Then, to complicate matters even more, I feel guilty about the boundaries I've set to survive. For instance, I don't go to office parties or activities such as games, sports, plays, fund-raisers, or weekend seminars."

Sara (sales clerk and mother of four): "I feel bad that I'm not there when my children get home from school. I'd like to hear all about their day, but by the time I'm home,

The Guilt Trip

the older ones have already explained the day's events to their friends over the telephone, and the younger ones have shared anything of interest with the babysitter. What they want from me is dinner."

I'm glad we don't deal with all of these issues simultaneously. If we did, few of us could continue. But what about moms who *are* dealing with one or more of these issues?

For those of us who are, guilt can feel like a rush of water barely held back by a dike with holes. Does the following example sound familiar?

At first she placed her finger in one lone hole to keep the guilt-water from leaking out and engulfing her. However, soon more leaks sprung in the dike. She busily stuck fingers into each hole until all of her fingers were occupied. More leaks began to spill out, so she plugged them with her toes, and the last one she filled with her tongue.

She found herself spread-eagle, robbed of strength and energy not to mention dignity. Although the awkwardness of her position caused her much pain, her great fear of the leaks forced her to stay. Numb and emotionally paralyzed, she pressed even tighter to her wall.

This example is extreme, but nearly all working moms encounter a form of the "Guilt Dam" at some point. For some of us, guilt is about as easy to "plug up" as it would be for us to part the Red Sea. Sure, that's been done, but not in our lifetimes.

THE WORKING MOTHER AND THE RED SEA CROSSING

Once, 120 years ago, there was a mother. She lived in the hills of North Dakota where her husband brought her as a young bride. She worked hard, and her days were full as she tended the garden, fed the chickens, milked the cow,

Sock Hunting and Other Pursuits

sewed, cooked, cleaned, and washed clothes in the creek.

Oftentimes, she did common things in new ways, for if they ran out of something, it could be many weeks before it could be obtained again. On days when things seemed impossibly hard, she reminded herself of a story her mother had told her as a child. She recalled the Israelites and their slavery in Egypt when their taskmasters said (speaking of the bricks they were required to make): *"You will not be given any straw, yet you must produce your full quota of bricks"* (Ex 5:10, paraphrased).

When she thought of this, she counted her blessings. For *she* had no cruel taskmaster standing over her. She was free. Her only "enemies" were the harsh sunlight of summer, the biting cold of winter, a tornado or two in the spring, and a few bugs and snakes in the fall. Over these she would prevail.

A town grew up around their homestead, and evenings were spent with other women sewing clothes for the needy.

Her daughters and their daughters lived on in the same way until the Depression of the 1930s, when a crop failure required them to sell much of their land.

Her husband was forced to get a job in the city. In their new home, she cooked, cleaned, and washed clothes in her wringer washing machine. Finances were tight. She could no longer go to her backyard and gather eggs or find a chicken to pluck; she spent more time and money in the grocery store. But whenever she felt pressured, she remembered her mother and the story of the Israelites who had to make bricks without straw.

Then, when her daughter grew and had a family of her own, things began to change. For her daughter became part of the nation's work force. In this way she helped ensure that her family had the straw necessary to make the bricks used in laying their financial foundation.

The Guilt Trip

Certain ones of society longed to "go back to the way it used to be"; back to the land of their former life. They called after her the way the Egyptians called after the Israelites, "Come back and serve us!"

She was treading new ground, and she knew it. The awesomeness of that knowledge sometimes wearied her, and she would pause to reflect. She would sometimes ask herself, "What am I doing this for?" At times it was even a little frightening. She remembered the story: *"[The children of Israel] said to Moses, 'Was it because there were no graves in Egypt that you brought us [here]?'"*

As she listened to the cries of some, "Come back—for you have transgressed!" she found herself camped by her own sea . . . a Sea of Guilt.

Then she remembered the words of Moses when the Israelites were pursued by the Egyptians: *"Do not be afraid. Stand firm . . . The Lord will fight for you while you keep silent."*

So she said nothing.

"Then the Lord said to Moses, 'Tell the Israelites to move on. Raise your staff and stretch out your hand over the sea to divide the water so that the Israelites can go through the sea on dry ground.'"

The WM looked out at the Sea of Guilt before her, and she heard the echoes of the questioning voices from behind. She gazed heavenward and cried out to her God, and she remembered the experience of Moses: *". . . the Lord drove the sea back with a strong east wind and turned it into dry land. The waters were divided, and the Israelites went through the sea on dry ground, with a wall of water on their right and on their left"* (see Exodus 14).

Then she heard the still small voice whisper, "There is now no condemnation for those who are in Christ Jesus" (Rom. 8:1). She felt great relief as she realized how to

Sock Hunting and Other Pursuits

handle the holes in the dike. "Go ahead, let your wall down," that voice continued. "I know it's scary, but only when that flimsy, woman-made wall comes down can God part the waters for you so you may cross over your own Sea . . . the Sea of Guilt."

She listened and obeyed the voice. Once she'd made a safe crossing, the waters again formed into a sea. The loving voice said to her, "This Sea is no longer called the Sea of Guilt. This is now the Sea of Forgetfulness, and all of your past wrongs, real or imagined, are buried there."

I'd like to say that once the WM got the inner issue of guilt resolved, she went merrily on her way, carefree and experiencing no anxious moments all the rest of her days. But you'd know better and so would I.

So, why did we just spend a good portion of this chapter discussing guilt? Because the rest is more a matter of wisdom than a matter of sin. What to do when, for how long and how much is a matter of personal and family priorities. However, these choices determine what kind of life we live, and unless we have resolved that inner guilt, we may lack the courage and strength to live out what we truly believe is important.

PRIORITIES

Alice says her children are the most important people in her life, but she feels guilty about how she treats them.

Alice, a mother of two boys under five, suffers from frequent pangs of guilt. Every morning she hustles around trying to get herself ready for work. She seldom has a chance to give the kids a bath and is lucky to even get their night diapers changed before she packs them up, straps them in the car, and runs them to the sitter.

The Guilt Trip

Alice leaves them clinging to the sitter, with whiny, runny noses, and wet diapers, relieved to have someone else cope with the mess. She goes to her job and puts in a full day's work. When she picks up her children they cry because they'd rather stay with the sitter. By the time she gets the kids home and supper on the table, she's spent.

Alice rushes through the bedtime routine with the children. Maybe she'll skip their baths tonight. After she puts them to bed, she can hear them crying in the other room. Guilt washes over her and she remembers somewhere that you can spoil a kid by rocking him to sleep once in a while. She doesn't dare start, they'd want it all the time, and she just couldn't.... Guilt nudges her but she shoves it aside and turns on her favorite television comedy for a few laughs.

She'll be glad when morning comes and she can drop off the kids again. At least at work, she's appreciated.

Alice *should* feel guilty, because she is neglecting her children. In order for the guilt feeling to go away, Alice must face it. She needs to examine the priorities in her life.[1]

Alice lives in a cycle. She neglects her children and then feels guilty. Guilt drains her of energy, and she arrives home tired night after night, the whole scenario repeating itself many times over.

Alice hasn't lived out her priorities. Because priorities stem from our basic value system, when we fail to live up to them, we violate those values and guilt is automatic.

SHADE OF GRAY

Cindy is also finding difficulty in carrying out the im-

Sock Hunting and Other Pursuits

portant things in her life, one of which is communication with her husband. She would say this is extremely vital to her, but her actions show otherwise.

Cindy arrives home after a long day, and her husband helps her cook dinner while the kids chatter about their activities. After dinner, her husband helps the kids with their homework, and Cindy does the dishes. While the kids dress for bed, her husband smiles and sighs as he drops onto the couch. Cindy heads for the dining room where she begins to polish the silver tray and pitcher that her mother gave to her.

"Cindy, why don't you come in here for a while?" her husband calls to her.

"I can't right now; I need to polish the silver. My mother is coming tomorrow."

Although Cindy would prefer a good long talk to cleaning the silver, she remembers that her mother cleaned that silver every two weeks. It has been a month and her mother's coming to visit.

Yet Cindy and her husband have both had a busy week. They've hardly had a conversation at all, other than bits and pieces while performing household tasks. What has happened to the priority of communication here? What's more important—the teapot or the husband?

On the other hand, we're not just talking about a teapot here. We're also talking about love as a mother hands down something precious to her daughter. Cindy's feeling of concern that she take care of something of value to her family is a valid one.

However, her uneasiness over her husband sitting alone in the living room when he wants to share time together must also be considered.

Perhaps the best approach to any conflict is honesty.

The Guilt Trip

Cindy could say something like this to her mother: "Mom, you know I've always thought that the silver tea set you handed down to me is beautiful. Even as a young girl, it was somehow a symbol of you. I've enjoyed having it, but I'm having a hard time taking proper care of it. Could you keep it for me until I'm able to give it the care it deserves?"

By saying this, Cindy runs the risk that the silver tea set will end up at her sister's house. Part of prioritizing is being able to risk losing some*thing* we enjoy for some*one* we love. To determine a priority, ask: What does God want for my life, and what am I prepared to sacrifice to attain or keep it?

Determining the necessary, the important, and the crucial, and exercising our options in order to carry those out, protects us from becoming like the battery-operated dancing flowers some stores carry. Someone turns them on, and someone turns them off. They have no minds, and they have no choice. The vibrations surrounding them determine their movements. Once purchased, they are a thing of amusement to show a friend. Otherwise, they sit in a corner where they are forgotten. They're not a major part of anyone's life.

Our choices count. When we sell ourselves short, we know it. We feel it. God in his grace forgives us. However, he also instructs us to "work out your salvation with fear and trembling" (Phil. 2:12). Could he be instructing us to choose and choose wisely?

One crucial area of choice is in what we choose to think about. When we have done wrong, acknowledged it, and God has forgiven us, we can focus our thoughts on his graciousness, not on our failures. He is our example. If he chooses to throw our sins and shortcomings into the Sea of Forgetfulness, we would do well to do the same.

While "time won't stand still long enough for us to

Sock Hunting and Other Pursuits

perfect our lives,"[2] we can accept God's invitation to "in all your ways acknowledge him and he will make your paths straight" (Prov. 3:6). We can be confident of his power to guide us as we choose. Then our guilt can give way to his assurance.

TIME TO CONSIDER

1. As a working mother, how can God help us through times of self-recrimination (Phil. 1:6; 3:9; Ps. 103:12)?

2. At those times when you wonder if you have the stamina to meet the needs of both job and home, what does God offer you (2 Cor. 3:5; 9:8; Phil. 4:13)? How is this practically applied?

3. What did God promise his worker in Genesis 28:15? How can we relate to this as working mothers today?

4. Guilt saps us of strength and energy. But what does God promise to us in Isaiah 40:31? What is he asking from us here? What does this tell us about spending time with God?

5

What's Realistic and What's Not?

As working mothers, we all want to do a good job in our dual role. One prominent author had this to say about us: "Mothers today place an extraordinary burden of expectation on themselves that they should be part Job, part Mary Poppins."[1]

If our own expectations aren't enough to overload us, we can always borrow some from the media. Elsa Houtz in *The Working Mother's Guide to Sanity* pokes fun at the media's portrayal of what a WM should be.

> If you buy a certain brand of peanut butter, milk, mayonnaise, cheese, or toilet paper, your family will know you love them. If you wear high heels at the office, don't expect to get ahead. Having clean, fresh-smelling clothes is of paramount importance to your loved ones. It's the least you can do for

Sock Hunting and Other Pursuits

them. Having clean, fresh-smelling carpets is of paramount importance to your loved ones. It's the least you can do for them. Never appear in public unless you are fully made up and wearing clothes that match. Your "I Climbed Pike's Peak" T-shirt and University of Tulsa running shorts do not constitute an ensemble. Your hairdo should last all day. So should you. If you are overtired or have the flu or sprain your ankle, that's no reason to slow down. Just take XYZ pharmaceutical products and you'll be able to remain standing, and maybe even breathing, all day.

Nothing hurts you. No demand on your time, energy, or emotions is too much. Nothing makes you sad or angry or frustrated. You can do anything. You're a working mother."[2]

Add to this the expectations we have of life and of those around us, and things can get complicated. Especially when it comes to our kids.

"With kids," it is said, "you have to expect the unexpected." When I first contemplated having children, I thought I could live with the unexpected. I'd learn to be flexible. I'd deal with it. I'd be a great parent! And in my heart, I meant it.

However, I hadn't bargained for certain aspects of parenting and holding down a job. For instance, who would have believed that after having children, we WMs might not sleep in again for another fifteen years? (At about age fifteen, when we'd like to see the kids up and at 'um early to do some yard work or help paint the house, all of their sleep mechanisms suddenly kick in.)

But during those years between birth and fifteen, there's not a chance of sleep—regardless if you've sound-proofed

What's Realistic and What's Not?

your room and barricaded your door. They'll find a way to get to you.

EXPECTATIONS AND SATURDAY MORNING

Six o'clock Saturday morning. You expect to sleep for another three hours. Your visit to oblivion includes a dream. You don't mind. It's a pleasant dream. You're sitting on a warm beach, and the soothing saltwater gently laps at your legs. A tropical breeze sweeps your hair back from your face. You take a bite of a huge, succulent strawberry, and its sweet citrus taste floods your mouth.

But—wait. Maybe you're not on a beach. Your mind gropes for consciousness. You are in your bed. And that warm water you feel? Not the ocean. Your son has migrated from his room to yours, and he straddles your thigh. "Mommy, I wet my bed." Then, as he blows on your face in an additional attempt to wake you, you are aware that this is no tropical breeze. And that taste in your mouth? It isn't strawberries. It's a resurrection of last night's pizza.

Just as disappointment sets in over the lost dream, you notice your husband snoring beside you and hope also builds. "I'm sure Daddy would like to know about this, too. Go tell Daddy."

Later that morning—after your son is clean and the sheets changed—you'd like to sip a cup of hot tea and read a magazine. But you won't. Your daughter needs a ride to the dress rehearsal for the play she's in tomorrow night. Sighing only slightly, you put down your magazine and console yourself. It's only a five-minute drive. The magazine will have to wait until you get back.

You see that your daughter is in her black dress and carrying the black scarf that will identify her as the play's widow woman. One last check to make sure she has

Sock Hunting and Other Pursuits

everything, you pile in the car, then stop by to pick up her friend. As she goes to the door to get Cindy, you congratulate yourself on how smoothly this is going. You're even on time.

You arrive at the rehearsal. "Oh, no! Mom, where's my scarf?" Your daughter rummages around in the front seat for a few seconds. "I think it fell out when we stopped to pick up Cindy!"

Inwardly you groan, but outwardly (as a dutiful mother) you say, "I'll go back and get it."

They go to their practice, and you drive back to the friend's house. You spot the scarf. But before the feeling of relief even registers, you size up the situation. The neighborhood boys have given the scarf to the neighborhood mutt, and they're trying to pull it out of his clenched teeth. They must have been at it for a while, because all that remains are a few tatters.

You consider having your daughter wear it anyway so that you can go back home and relax. After all, she *is* playing the part of a poor widow woman. However, as you get out of the car to retrieve the scarf, the dog squats. One of the boys yanks the scarf from the mutt's clenched teeth. He drops it, then steps on it. As you move closer and realize what he has dropped it on and mashed it into, you hustle to your car before anyone insists that the scarf is yours.

Now you're minus the scarf, and the play is tomorrow. You decide that the magazine will have to wait a few more minutes as you head to the store. One store turns into four and four stores turn into nine. Have you ever tried to find a solid black scarf when you need one?

Finally, on the twenty-third try, you spot a lone black scarf. Two elderly ladies are also screening the scarf rack. But you (with absolutely no twinge of guilt) rush over and

What's Realistic and What's Not?

grab the ugly thing before either one of them has a chance to reach for it. As if it were an Anne Klein original marked down low enough so you could afford it, you hurry to the cash register before anyone has time to protest.

By now dress rehearsal is over, and it's time to pick up your daughter. After all you've been through this morning, you expect her to run to you and say, "Thank you, Mom, thank you. You're the greatest mom in the whole world!" Instead, she says, "Mom, you're almost ten minutes late. And you never did come back with my scarf."

Some expectations will never be met. The more we invest in them the more we lose. The more important we allow them to become, the worse we feel if our hopes aren't realized.

EXPECTATIONS OF OURSELVES

A few years ago I failed to meet a couple of expectations for myself. Actually, I've messed up on hundreds of self-inflicted demands. As you'll see, I've gotten over a couple well enough to talk about them. Instead of admitting failure and learning to live with it or starting over, I invested more and more.

It started on a rainy Saturday afternoon. With the morning chores completed, my husband Tim and I talked about what to do with the rest of the afternoon.

"What do you want to do?" I asked.

"I don't know, what do you want to do?" We both hate making decisions on Saturdays.

"How about taking the kids to pizza?"

"Not a bad idea except for the other zillion kids that'll be there. Why don't we save that for a Tuesday evening sometime?"

"Okay." I didn't really want to fight the crowds, either. "Let's stay home; after lunch we can watch an old movie,

Sock Hunting and Other Pursuits

and I'll bake chocolate chip cookies."

"Sounds good to me. I'll build a fire."

Later, as I dropped the cookie dough onto the pan, it seemed a bit goopy. I baked a few to see how they would turn out. When I pulled them from the oven, they were as thin as silver dollars and the bottoms were black.

I normally bake good cookies, and I wasn't willing to settle for these crispy critters. Especially when my husband looked right at them and said, "When are you going to bake the cookies?" After shooing him out of the kitchen, I decided that a little more flour would certainly transform this mess into yummy, soft Toll House cookies.

I began to pour. After making my additions, I baked a few cookies. This time they came out looking and tasting more like bread with chocolate chips. This wasn't the effect I was looking for, so I decided that with all that extra flour, they probably needed an equal amount of sugar. I baked a few that way, but they came out hard and dry. Then a friend dropped by.

"Why don't you add a couple of eggs?" she said as she eyed the heavy lumps. The batch had grown to nearly double its size, so I also added more chocolate chips.

When I pulled these out of the oven, they were still somewhat flat. My husband offered: "With all that extra stuff you put in, did you add any baking soda?"

No, I hadn't.

So, when I added the baking soda, I also came across the salt . . . maybe two or three extra teaspoons couldn't hurt.

The oven timer rang, and I set this batch carefully on the counter. I felt confident. They had the perfect texture. They were an even golden brown. When Tim broke one apart the half-melted chocolate chips oozed out just right. I waited as he bit into one of my masterpieces of dessert delicacy.

"Ugh, how much salt did you put in these things?"

What's Realistic and What's Not?

I tasted. Sure enough, they were so salty I could have used them to season a soup.

I had too much invested in them to quit, so we decided to double the recipe (all except the salt). Then the salt level should be just perfect, right?

By Monday the dough would no longer fit into our refrigerator so we stored it in the garage in a big plastic tub. And it was still awful stuff.

I don't remember if we picked the chocolate chips out and reused them, baked the mess and ate it, or disposed of the whole thing. Perhaps if I could recall the consequences of this incident I wouldn't have carried this particular tendency into the workplace, investing time and energy into unrealistic expectations in the mistaken belief that "I can make it work."

Haven't we been taught all our lives that "there's no virtue in quitting"? So, sometimes it's hard to let go, admit a mistake, and move on. The "never admit defeat" principle definitely worked against me in the chocolate chip department—and the employment sector.

ONE WORKING MOM'S BLUES

Until my first child was three, I worked in sales and sales management. It was fast-paced and had its moments of pressure, but I enjoyed the challenge. Then I became pregnant with my second child. The added responsibility of preparing for a new baby plus caring for my first child and working a job caused the pressure that I'd once considered a challenge to become just pressure to me. I quit working to have my second child and decided that when I returned I'd find something more low-key.

When I did reenter the work force, I took an entry-level, twenty-hour-a-week position. I made one-fifth what I'd made before. The twenty hours turned out to be mostly

Sock Hunting and Other Pursuits

evenings and weekends, and the company expected me to be on-call any additional day they needed me. My twenty-hour-a-week job quickly turned into a thirty-six-hour-a-week job, with none of the benefits I once had. My whole life operated around a job that paid practically nothing. Not to mention my boss, who was as easy to get along with as Attila the Hun.

But I *wasn't* going to quit. After all, I hadn't worked in several years. It wouldn't look good on my resume to have quit this job after only a short time. Yet, I had never worked while mothering more than one child. Maybe I couldn't do it. No, I reasoned, if I stay and they know I can do a good job, I'm sure things will change.

I stayed, but things didn't change. I became more and more unhappy and my attitude deteriorated. But I *wasn't* going to quit!

Finally, they fired me. I was devastated.

Here I'd managed a business, and now I was told I couldn't handle an entry-level position. I had expected to make this work.

With my pride severely wounded, I wondered what to do. I knew that financially I needed to work, and I knew I didn't want anything so intense that I had nothing left to give my family at the end of the day. I began to pray, but I was afraid to look again. I feared another disaster.

A month later, I remembered an account executive who used to call on the company where I worked part-time. I contacted her and let her know I was looking for work.

Two weeks later she informed me of an opening in her company. It paid twice what I had been making, and the hours were perfect.

I've been there ever since and love the work and the people. Had I not been forced to release my expectation that the first job would work out, I wouldn't have discov-

What's Realistic and What's Not?

ered a job that *did* work.

Expectations are what we'd *like* to happen or what we think *should* happen. Yet our expectations may not be the best for us, and they're certainly not holy writ. We must learn to be flexible, or they'll crush us.

When we invest so highly in a dead-end, we have little energy left to do anything else. If we consistently fall short of our self-imposed requirements and find it difficult to fulfill the requests of others, it's time to examine our expectations and the wishes of those around us. Do they make sense? Are they productive? Is there a reason behind them? If you're like me, sometimes the answer to all three of these questions is no.

For instance, is it necessary to make homemade bread if you don't have time? What is the benefit of keeping house like the cover of *House Beautiful* if this activity leaves you tired, irritable, and frustrated? What's wrong with a floor that got swept today instead of mopped yesterday? What is the virtue in smiling brightly and saying, "Sure, I'll help you make uniforms for the boy's club," if you're already stretched beyond human capacity? Wouldn't it be better to offer to pay someone to sew them?

Someone from church calls and asks, "Will you teach a Sunday school class for three months?" This is a worthy thing to do and help if you can. But if you are struggling to find meaningful time with your family and your Creator, isn't it better to say, "No, I can't do that right now"?

I'm not suggesting to working mothers that service to God and others should be eliminated. Quite the opposite. Budget these services into your schedule. If you are confident that you are already doing what you can, this will help alleviate guilt feelings if you need to refuse a request.

I've often come face-to-face with requests I couldn't fulfill. I wanted to help and felt guilty saying no, especially

Sock Hunting and Other Pursuits

when others encouraged me to join in projects they were involved in. Frustration mounted until I honestly began saying, "You know, what you're doing is a really good thing. You're involved in a powerful way, and I can see God is directing you. However, a lot is happening right now, and I can't be involved in everything. If I were, I wouldn't have time to do the things I believe God wants me to do." I then listed areas I felt were priorities.

While not everyone understood (and they won't with you, either), this clarified what I was willing and able to do. Once said, the other person will either appreciate what you *are* doing or become upset over what you *aren't* doing. Remember, we are responsible for our actions and choices. We are not responsible for how the other person acts or reacts.

Most people will understand and accept what you have to offer. However, some may insist that if a cause is worthy of their attention, it's worthy of yours, as well. Often these people feel threatened. Their "project" may have an exaggerated importance in their lives due to a lack or a need in another area, and they may interpret your refusal to help as a personal rejection.

As much as we may want to, we will never fill every need for every person. But, if we are "living purposefully, worthily, accurately . . . being sensible, intelligent, and wise in the rationing of our time,"[3] we will be likened to the woman who broke the jar of perfume over Jesus' head. The disciples criticized what she had to offer, saying she should have done something else. But Jesus had quite a different opinion. He said simply, "Leave her alone. . . . Why are you bothering her? She has done a beautiful thing to me. . . . She did what she could" (Mark 14:6, 8).

Charles Swindoll in *Come Before Winter* lists specific areas of frustration that hinder us:

What's Realistic and What's Not?

- attempting too much at once
- setting unrealistic time estimates
- procrastinating
- failing to determine specific priorities
- failing to listen well
- failing to delegate
- failing to write things down
- possessing an inability to say no
- focusing on needless details
- lacking organization
- a reluctance to get started
- an absence of self-appointed deadlines
- not doing first things first [4]

Unwise or unrealistic planning doesn't help us get more done. In fact, it may promote *lower* productivity. When we plan more than is humanly possible to deliver, we set ourselves up for frustration. Frustration is either vented outwardly, which takes time and energy, or inwardly, robbing us of the buoyancy that enables us to produce.

A fine line exists between *faith* that prompts us to accomplish what others thought impossible and *stubbornness* that enslaves us, forcing us to invest so heavily in what we wish were possible that we miss out on what we *can* accomplish. Such as maintaining an inner peace that passes all understanding and survives even the ruins of our unmet expectations.

TIME TO CONSIDER

1. Why do you think Jesus said what he did in Matthew 11:29, 30?

2. How can we apply the above concept in our efforts to fulfill our responsibilities as mothers/workers? How can we apply this to our service to God and others?

Sock Hunting and Other Pursuits

3. How can these verses guide us as we set our goals and make our plans?

4. What kinds of expectations can we have of God (Ps. 73:23, 24; Prov. 30:5; John 14:26; Rom. 8:38, 39; James 1:17; 1 John 3:2, 3)? What does God expect from us (Micah 6:8; Matt. 22:27-29; 2 Pet. 3:18)?

5. Whose hopes are realized? Whose expectations perish (Prov. 10:28; 11:7, 23)? What can we do with those unrealistic expectations we either put on ourselves or let others put on us?

6

High Wires and Teeter-Totters

Many mothers have outgrown the superwoman approach to working/mothering and no longer balance on a high wire ("no matter how difficult things become, I can single-handedly balance them on a thin wire of steel high above the crowd; you may see me teeter, but you'll never see me fall"). Many of us left that show behind at the circus where it belongs. Although our balancing act may have looked successful in the workplace, we found the results at home too devastating. When we perched ourselves on the high wire of "I can do it alone," we became unreachable to our families. It was lonely and scary up there, honing our act, while our loved ones ate popcorn and talked to each other down below.

Yes, most of us have come down to earth. Some of us fell down. Some climbed down willingly when we outgrew the need to show off. But although we may be closer

Sock Hunting and Other Pursuits

to having our feet planted firmly on the ground, and for the most part have resisted the tendency to become the "Rambo" of working womanhood, we may still encounter some heavy-duty balancing feats. Mothers of the nineties often find themselves straddling a teeter-totter.

Mindy sometimes feels like that. The seat on one end of the teeter-totter is work. The seat on the other end is home. The middle is motherhood. As a WM, Mindy straddles the middle zone in an endeavor to maintain a balance. She struggles to get to work on time and feed her kids a good healthy breakfast. She wonders how she can go to the scholar of the month assembly tomorrow where her son will be honored, when the school just *now* called to inform her of it, and she's scheduled to work.

She finds herself on this teeter-totter again when her day off rolls around, and she'd prefer to do something deliciously fun, but the house desperately needs cleaning and her family hasn't had a homemade meal in two weeks.

At times like these either the home seat or work seat begins to feel overloaded, causing her to slide, on a rather rough plank, toward one end or the other. Slivers jab her and threaten to penetrate the most calloused skin of WM determination that says, "I can handle it."

The growing number of mothers in the work force are seeking to learn how to manage their time. The idea is to squeeze the maximum amount of productivity, family satis-faction, and leisure into the minimum amount of time. This approach can often lead to as many questions as answers.

- How do we work and have a personal life at the same time?
- When do we work and when do we relax?
- How can we be productive at work while nurturing a family at home?

High Wires and Teeter-Totters

Many WMs, in their attempt to not only answer these questions but put the answers into practice, find themselves on that emotional teeter-totter with Mindy.

Although this is painful, it also alerts us when our lives are genuinely off center. Our response to this knowledge determines what happens next. We choose to react in one of two ways. We either: 1. quit our jobs and put all our effort into the home seat; or 2. give up hope of any kind of order in our personal lives and lean more and more heavily into our work, leaving a void in our homes.

The trouble with the first reaction is that while it may alleviate frustration in one area, it creates other problems. Many of us work for financial reasons—our families are truly in need. Our pressured decision to stay home may put a financial burden upon our household that could have a negative effect equivalent to the pressure we felt as WMs. If this happens, we come no closer to reaching family balance.

If a single mother quits her job, it's doubtful that she will find the lack of income or the possibility of welfare any easier than the endeavor to juggle both job and family.

The mother who embraces the second reaction enjoys the orderliness of work and the satisfaction of completing certain tasks before going on to others. The constant demands of home and mothering appear a raw deal in comparison. She tends to come into work early and stay late, making herself unavailable to her family. While she spends more and more time away, her home becomes increasingly disorganized and her children (because they feel neglected) more demanding. Her desire to be at home decreases.

What are the answers? If our reactions to circumstances don't bring about the balance we desire, what will?

Sock Hunting and Other Pursuits

IDENTIFY THE CONFLICT

When something is off center—just doesn't feel right—we often move on instead of admitting to a pattern. After all, we're working moms. We don't have slots of time available for self-reflection, right?

But this refusal to deal with our feelings or the feelings of others leads in one basic direction. At some point, one end or the other of that teeter-totter becomes so off balance that it crashes to the ground, leaving us in a great deal of emotional or even physical pain.

We know that one end is overloaded when we feel excessive stress.

STRESS

Stress is pressure, force, strain, or great effort. Ulcers, colitis, frequent headaches, back pain, and some digestive disorders are only a few of the ailments that are associated with stress. Doctors and scientists are currently researching possible links to more illnesses and physical symptoms believed to be caused by stress.

A popular women's magazine, in cooperation with Dr. Deborah Belle, recently did a study to pinpoint specific areas of stress that working moms experience. Some of the stress factors in our lives may be:

1. You don't have enough money to meet your family's needs.

2. Your husband doesn't do a fair share of the housework.

3. You work at a low-paying, dead-end job.

4. You have recently separated, divorced, or been widowed.

5. Your parents or other close relatives live no more than a 15-minute drive away from you.

High Wires and Teeter-Totters

6. You live in a high-crime area.

7. You rely on an unpaid relative or friend for child care.

8. Your job is boring and repetitive.

9. You've had a major health problem in the last year.

10. You work more than 55 hours a week at your job(s).

11. You are dissatisfied with the quality of the child care arrangement you currently have.

12. You have no close friends nearby in your community.

13. You don't have an advanced education or specialized training. You'd like to get ahead on the job.

14. Your job makes it tough for you to take time off to attend to your child's appointments or other needs.[1]

While these life situations (the biggies) can cause stress, it's often the details that produce even more tension. You may identify with many of the following:

> Your neighbor won't babysit for you.
>
> Your husband is going out of town this Friday and won't be available to pick your daughter up at the child-care center.
>
> Your son's teacher calls you at the office to inform you that, for the third day in a row, Ricky has wet his pants.
>
> You have more and more trouble getting out of the house on time in the morning.
>
> You receive this month's bank statement and realize that your last five checks are going to bounce.
>
> Your child's before-and-after school program is closing this week.
>
> Your boss wants you to stay late tonight and you can't.
>
> Your in-home caregiver has called in sick again.

Sock Hunting and Other Pursuits

Your child tells you it's okay, he doesn't mind if you miss the spring carnival at school this Thursday.[2]

To observers we may look as if we have it all together (a good job, terrific family, etc.). But with all the stress points, we're all too aware of the extreme effort we exert. Sometimes that awareness (when it weighs us down) can cause us to fail to take pleasure in *any* of it. While we believe we are simply reacting to the difficulties, sometimes our reaction can indicate an added dilemma—self-reproach.

SELF-REPROACH

Self-reproach among working mothers runs high and wide. They feel guilty for going back to work "too soon" after the birth of a child *and* for taking a leave of absence from a job, for staying at the office late to catch up on a backlog of work *and* for leaving early to take care of a family matter. Like a burr, guilt attaches itself to working mothers' lives, making it all but impossible for them to derive satisfaction from *any* decision or action they take.[3]

Have you ever felt like this? I have. Some of the things we do at these times can exacerbate the situation even further. For instance, when we feel self-reproach because our children aren't receiving the same type of mothering we did (a home cooked meal every night, a spotless home to enjoy and invite their friends to, and a mother who attends all school functions), we can tend to overcompensate.

We overextend ourselves to please our children to make up for going to work. We may go out of our way to do something for our child when we don't really have time, and we become frustrated and grumpy—jeopardizing what time we do have with our child. It's so easy to get caught up in grandiose efforts so our child will feel loved. Oftentimes, what the child would really like is to see Mom relax, smile, and enjoy herself with them.

Sometimes we can be our own worst enemy. When we allow self-reproach to envelop us, it may encroach upon our work life.

Self-reproach over leaving our children can cause us to stretch out the morning as long as possible . . . as we *slowly* get ready for work. We *slowly* get our children to the sitter. We're late, and our boss is unhappy. Then we feel guilty about being late *and* leaving our children. We may procrastinate at work or participate in self-defeating behavior in an effort to punish ourselves.

SELF-EXAMINATION

Are we really participating in self-defeating patterns? We can ask ourselves four basic questions to find out.

1. Am I consistently late for work?
2. Do I procrastinate while I'm there?
3. Do I often excuse why I couldn't get something done?
4. Do I fail to keep up on new procedures and products that would help me in my job?

If the answer to any of these questions is yes, take a few moments to consider: "Why am I working? Do I believe in what I'm doing? Do I believe this job is helping my family? Is this job part of God's provision for my family?"

If you still feel confident about working after answering these questions, then recognize that Jesus said, ". . . know the truth, and the truth will set you free" (John 8:32). We don't have to lock ourselves into self-devaluing behavior.

As WMs we will face some sticky choices. Uncomfortable choices. But discomfort doesn't always mean that we are in the wrong place at the wrong time. It may just mean we need God's wisdom and help.

The pit that Joseph's brothers threw him into did not come equipped with padded cushions and tropical drinks to sip (Gen. 37:12-28). Of course not. It was a slimy hole and extremely uncomfortable. But had he not been there at that time, he wouldn't have been sold to the Midianites. He wouldn't later have become Pharaoh's overseer of the food during a famine and had provisions to offer his family in their need. He was often uncomfortable, but his discomfort didn't mean he was in the wrong place at the wrong time. He was right where he needed to be, asking for and receiving God's help in the midst of difficult times and situations.

What a great place for us to be today as WMs. For it is only as we humble ourselves and seek his wisdom and direction that he promises to provide us with both. In Jeremiah, God promises, "I know the plans I have for you ... plans to prosper you and not to harm you" (Jer. 29:11).

However, even with God's guidance, working moms face a lot of hard work. God isn't going to do my dishes for me or show up at work in my stead. He's not going to circulate an office memo on time or pull the clothes out of the dryer when the buzzer rings. To accomplish these tasks, often simultaneously, I must plan as well as learn how to delegate.

In the home and workplace, planning is putting God's wisdom into action, sometimes with profound effects.

A PLAN TO IMPROVE PERFORMANCE

A significant factor in our stress level is our perceived ability to improve the situations that trouble us. Improvement, whether a change in circumstances or an attitude shift, doesn't happen by accident. Only accidents happen by accident. While God calls for improvement (he is changing us each day from glory to glory, [2 Cor. 3:18 KJV]), improvement calls for action.

The following worksheet was designed by Dr. Renee Y. Magid, president and founder of Initiatives, The Center for the Advancement of Work and Family. She has also written several books, including *When Mothers and Fathers Work*. This chart will help us in our action planning.

PLAN OF ACTION WORKSHEET

I. Area for Consideration (e.g. child care, relocation):
_____
_____

II. Goal (I want to achieve the following):
_____
_____

III. Target Completion Date for Reaching This Goal:
_____
_____

IV. Action Steps Necessary to Reach This Goal (include as many as you feel necessary):

Action Steps	Beginning Target Date	Date Actually Completed
1. _____	_____	_____
2. _____	_____	_____
3. _____	_____	_____
4. _____	_____	_____
5. _____	_____	_____

V. Reviewing and Monitoring Progress

You need to decide how often you will monitor your progress. Some goals require daily monitoring, while others may require a weekly or monthly review.

1. Will I reach my goal by my beginning target date?
2. If not, what may be hindering me?

Sock Hunting and Other Pursuits

Need more ability in _____
_____.

Need more knowledge of _____
_____.

Goal is not consistent with my overall plan_____
_____.

Fear of success of failure in _____
_____.

Goal is more difficult than I foresaw because _____
_____.

Goal is unrealistic in light of my current work/family commitments _____
_____.

Goal is achievable, but original target date was unrealistic _____
_____.

Other _____
_____.

3. Do I want to continue to reach this goal? _____.
4. Do I need or want to revise my goal? _____.
5. If so, rewrite goal, action steps, and target dates on another page . . . [4]

Permission must be granted to duplicate this form if it is used for any purpose other than a personal one.

TIME TO CONSIDER

1. With the varied aspects and interests of a two-parent employed household, what will it take to bring a healthy balance according to Hebrews 12:11? Be specific.

2. In what areas of your life can you apply this Hebrews 12:11 principle? Can you think of specific ways this philosophy can benefit you and your family today?

High Wires and Teeter-Totters

3. The instructions in Hebrews 12:12, 13 sound almost harsh to one who is broken or overburdened. Yet read the last part of this verse. In what areas of your emotions and will do you need to be healed?

4. What was David's response to the complexities of his world (Ps. 55:6)? Have you ever felt like this? Has an airplane bound for "anywhere but here" looked good to you in the past few months? If so, feel free to be honest and acknowledge your true feelings. But then notice the action that David took in the first part of Psalm 55:16.

5. In times of imbalance and distress, we have the ability to instruct our soul (Ps. 62:5). How can this ability be advantageous to us as WMs?

7

Help! The Ravenous Multitude Is after Me

One challenge of the working mom's life is taking charge of what I call "food for the ravenous multitude." What's the problem? Nothing, really. Except that we're tired at the end of the day, and our families still want to eat.

A typical day goes something like this:

Due to unforeseen circumstances, you're twenty minutes late getting off work. A broken stoplight has traffic snarled for at least a mile. That mile takes longer than the entire trip home normally does.

If you wear heels and stand all day, your back and feet hurt. If you type, file, or do administrative work, your head aches.

You walk into the house; your husband and kids have just arrived home. "What's for dinner?" your oldest child asks.

Sock Hunting and Other Pursuits

"Dinner?" Your scrambled thoughts try to collect themselves and shift gears. "Dinner. Let's see, what did I take out of the freezer this morning?" A quick examination of the bare countertop and sink reveals nothing. You took nothing out of the freezer this morning.

With a groan, you go quickly to the refrigerator. Any suitable leftovers?

"What did you say we're having, Mom?"

"Ugh, I'm still looking."

"Mom, Billy's family eats at 4:30. How come we don't eat till 6:00?"

You try to ignore your child as you begin to pull Tupperware from the refrigerator. "If we each have something different, I think we can feed everyone."

On one such night, this is how we handled mealtime. My oldest daughter Amee got leftover ham and mashed potatoes. I cut up a salad. My middle daughter Rachel ate leftover spaghetti. My youngest Joel got stuck with leftover tacos. My husband Tim added shrimp to the salad and put a couple of potatoes in the microwave. We all drank grape juice.

Sound simple enough? It is. Except for the timing of it. Dinner comes directly after work . . . after work when a hot tub and food brought on a tray sounds more in order.

Instead, as a working mom, I sometimes feel like the ravenous multitude is after me. In fact, on certain days I've even felt a little like Moses.

MOSES AND ME

No, I'm not leading a great army of people through the desert to the land of promise. I'm only a working mom, trying to nurture my three children in the ways of the Lord. But, like Moses when he led his band of thousands through the desert, I am weary of the responsibility of

Help! The Ravenous Multitude Is after Me

feeding them on the run.

The children of Israel soon became sick of manna. My children are sick of Mom's cooking. (I only know how to make five things quickly, three of which they hate.)

"The crowd that followed Moses into the desert lusted for the dainty food of Egypt: melons, fish, onions, and garlic." My children lust for the good old days when Mom didn't work and made everything from whole wheat bread to ketchup from scratch. The children of Israel didn't recognize that along with the dainty morsels back in Egypt, they were also held in bondage. My children don't understand that in my pre-working days, we not only had the dainty morsels but some financial bondage as well. Alas, our family couldn't live on bread alone. To keep up with the needs of a growing family whose income hadn't grown at quite the same rate, I found myself working.

That's when my cooking troubles began.

I collect all the "quick" recipes I can find and use time-saving tips and appliances, but when I dutifully try to cook, I still end up with bread that falls apart. It's probably good that it tastes so awful—it saves us the torture of trying to eat it. When I fix breakfast, my husband looks in the pan and says, "Don't fix a thing for me, Honey. I'll just grab a doughnut." Or (I love this one), "I think I'll fast today."

"The children of Israel said to Moses, 'There is nothing at all to eat, well, besides this manna.'" My children exaggerate even more. "We're starving to death. There's absolutely nothing to eat." They don't even give me credit for the mess on their plate. At least I tried. Can I help it if I'm not Julia Child?

"And Moses heard the people weeping throughout their families . . . and in the eyes of Moses it was evil." And I heard my children crying for anybody's cooking but mine,

Sock Hunting and Other Pursuits

and it was evil in the sight of me.

"Then Moses says to the Lord, 'I am not able to carry all these people alone, because the burden is too heavy for me.'" I say, "Lord, give me a maid who cooks."

"Then Moses says, 'And if this is the way you deal with me, kill me, I pray you, at once and be granting me a favor.'" I don't get quite that depressed. "Lord, give us manna again so I don't have to cook."

"Then Moses says, 'And let me not see the wretchedness in the failure of all my efforts.'" I say, "Oh, hang it. If they really tried, they could probably eat the crummy stuff."

"And the Lord said to Moses, 'Gather for me seventy men of the elders of Israel . . . and they shall bear the burden of the people with you, so that you may not have to bear it yourself alone.'" "Yippee! Lord, does this mean I can have a maid who cooks?" I reach for the yellow pages and flip to the M's for "Maid Service," when the still small voice from within says, "No, turn to schools." I think, "Isn't that just like you, Lord! You're going to find me a maid who's just getting out of maid school—one who's extremely talented. Thank you."

"Then Moses says to God: 'Why have you dealt ill with your servant and why have I not found favor in your sight, that you lay all the burden of all these people on me. Have I conceived these people?'" To his last question, I have to answer, "Yes, I guess I did."

"Have I brought them forth that you should say to me, 'Carry them in your bosom?'" [1] Yes, I guess I did that, too.

As I turn the page to schools, the only thing that stands out is "Busy Woman's School of Cooking." This time that quiet voice fully breaks through. "LEARN HOW TO COOK ON THE RUN."

Help! The Ravenous Multitude Is after Me

I have since learned to cook a little more quickly and efficiently. However, cooking at the end of the day when everyone is tired and hungry is still a challenge.

I have found a few things helpful in keeping a family fed after five o'clock.

THREE P'S TO MAXIMIZE TIME

Plan

In her book, *Massive Meal Planning*, Linda Moxley explains, "I only cook one day every month and a half." Quite an unusual statement considering Linda has seven children. No, they aren't rich. Linda plans ahead.

On cooking day, she cooks twenty pounds of hamburger in a giant pot, divides it up, and freezes it. Next, Linda boils twenty pounds of chicken, picks it off the bone, and puts it into freezer bags. Then she grates three pounds each of mozzarella, cheddar, and swiss cheeses. She bags and freezes those. Often-used vegetables such as green bell peppers, mushrooms, and onions can also be frozen.[2]

This preparation makes fixing a meal more a matter of assembling a dish than cooking and it frees valuable time for other things.

Though this method may not be for everyone, some preparation the night before can make the difference between chaos or calm come dinnertime.

"She gets up while it is still dark; she provides food for her family. . . . She sees that her trading is profitable, and her lamp does not go out at night" (Prov. 31:15, 18). By planning the following day's menu the night before, ample opportunity is available to check the cupboards to ensure that you have the ingredients you need. If something is missing, you can ask a family member to go to the market. My thirteen-year-old enjoys grocery shopping for me. She

Sock Hunting and Other Pursuits

calls a couple of friends, and they walk or ride bikes together. I always give them a little extra money for a few pieces of licorice or something.

Every couple of weeks, I bake a large batch of bran muffins and freeze them. It take minutes to mix them and put them in the oven. Reheated in the microwave, they make healthy snacks for kids (or adults!) who can't wait for dinner.

These are a few practical suggestions. However, I'm well aware that no matter how carefully we plan, evening meals still take extra effort and energy.

Along with the challenge, reward yourself now and then. We eat out at least once a week. It doesn't have to be an expensive restaurant. Sometimes we take the kids to pizza; or my husband and I leave the kids home (it's great to have a daughter of baby-sitting age). After eating, we linger and talk for a while. Uninterrupted mealtime is a gift of God.

Once every few weeks, plan an evening with friends. Go shopping, eat dinner out, or find a hot tub and just sit in it. You'll be a happier person. Your husband and kids will manage the evening without you. They may even enjoy knowing you had a good time. Don't look at these evenings as selfishness on your part, just rejoice that they're possible. Knowing you have a treat coming will lessen the pressure when you're feeling bogged down.

But even when we take care of ourselves in these ways, how do we deal with the frustration of the moment; we don't want to cook, but we must cook?

Sometimes I've dealt with this successfully; sometimes not so successfully. At times I've been reduced to a screaming shrew. "Why don't you do dinner?" I've shouted at no one in particular.

Emilie Barns in *More Hours in My Day* writes, "We by

Help! The Ravenous Multitude Is after Me

ourselves cannot do it all in our homes (when we try we become frustrated), so when we begin to delegate responsibilities to our children and allow them to do some of the work for us, they begin to feel as if they are a vital part of the family. I have found that families that work together and play together will also love together, pray together, and worship God together. Then we'll raise children who are balanced people, who will become creative adults with wonderful homes of their own."[3]

I've used this principle in our home and am happy with the results in most areas. However, in the kitchen and meal preparation, success has been minimal.

My girls are old enough to set the table and load the dishwasher. But the cooking?

My oldest daughter is athletic and couldn't care less about domestic activities. She has many talents and abilities but little or no cooking aptitude. She is involved in sports and often gets home later than I do.

My younger daughter has the aptitude and desire but not the motor skills needed for meal preparation. Flour doesn't land in the bowl, it lands on the floor and cabinets. An egg, once it's broken, lands only partially on target. The rest oozes its way off the counter into an open drawer. "Oops," I hear a dozen times when she cooks.

Then she calls me in when she's all finished. "Mom, come look what I made."

I keep the smile on my face when I see the dumped over containers, their contents splattered far and wide. Stubbornly that smile even remains when my foot crunches something on the floor. It fades only slightly when my next step sends me skidding down onto my overloaded posterior.

"Mommy, are you okay?" Rachel comes to help me up.

"I think so," I say, but I wonder if I'm lying.

Sock Hunting and Other Pursuits

When I finally get onto my feet, my clothes soiled and my body still in pain, my little one points to the ruins. "See, Mom? I followed your recipe for muffins."

As I look at the pan and view its sunken contents, I also notice the dough that it sits on. By now it is stuck to the countertop. My eyes blur a little bit with tears. I wonder—tears of pride or tears of pain? No, I *am* proud. "Just look at what my little girl has made," I repeat.

But, alas, no matter how proud I am, it's too much work to have my daughter cook very often.

The other option is my husband. Now there's a treat. Yes, my husband can cook. He is willing to cook. He *does* cook. However, this option brings up some problems. He has no concern for calories. He doesn't need to. He's five-feet ten-inches tall and weighs one hundred-seventy pounds. He hasn't any idea what a calorie is and he still looks great.

Unfortunately, if I approached food like that, I'd also weigh one hundred-seventy pounds—but I only stand five-feet three-inches. Hmm. . . .

Besides, he's a pastor and often unavailable at the cooking hour. Let's face it, making tuna casserole doesn't take precedence over a parishioner in deep need.

So for now, most of the cooking goes to me. We can talk about equal responsibilities, but things are still the way they are. Many women, for one reason or another, are still the primary cook.

One author commented, "While there has been rapid growth in women's participation in the work force, division of labor has changed slowly or not at all."[4]

Dinner always comes at the end of the day when people are tired and hungry. It's one of the uglier facts of life. But along with planning we can also prioritize.

Help! The Ravenous Multitude Is after Me

Prioritize

"Accept the fact that you are limited to 24 hours. Set realistic goals. Forget perfection—aim for flexibility. Accept your human limitations and avoid a 'But I should be able to' mentality. Don't be a martyr—accept help if it's offered. Take time to enjoy your family even if it means some task goes undone. Accept necessary 'trade-offs.' If you've volunteered to provide cookies for a class party but find yourself in a real time bind, buy the cookies rather than decorate them. It will mean more to your child to be dropped off at school with a smile on your face and a 'Have a great party, Honey,' than for you to have spent hours decorating cookies and dropping them off at school with a hassled expression and an implied 'I hope you're happy' attitude."[5]

When we do this, we're prioritizing. We can also learn to take pleasure in mealtimes.

Pleasure

Taking pleasure in mealtimes is possible. Even on a limited time schedule, a limited budget, and limited energy, mealtime can be enjoyed. If I had any doubts before, a recent trip to Romania and other eastern European countries put perspective on my dinnertime blues. Although many positive changes have occurred since I visited, seeing their hardship caused me to question my own approach to mealtime.

In these societies, women were encouraged, even forced, to work outside the home. Add to that time pressure the fact that food was rationed, and many foods could only be purchased in commodity lines. If a woman wanted milk, she stood in line for it at 5:30 A.M. Bread was obtained in the same manner. After work she stood in another line for cheese, if it were available. Meat was nearly never available.

Sock Hunting and Other Pursuits

Yet these women reveled in mealtime. Why? Why would so little, purchased with so much effort, bring such a refreshing time of support?

Is an oppressive communist dictatorship the formula for family mealtime enjoyment. Surely not.

Is it because they are Christians? I'm a Christian, too, but often dinnertime at my house leaves me feeling tired and hassled. As important as faith is, there had to be more.

Maybe it is because they often entertain guests, I rationalized. That's when the Holy Spirit probed me to look a little deeper, and I began to ask myself pointed questions.

Could their mealtime pleasure have anything to do with the fact that dinner was the evening's main event? I thought of all the times I've rushed through mealtime to get to church, do some "needed" shopping, or take a hot bath.

Or perhaps there, no one wanted to scarf down dinner so they could watch their favorite TV show. (At the time we visited Romania, TV consisted of speeches by their dictator, telling of *his* beautiful Romania and all he had done for her. No one rushed through anything to watch him. There was no need to rush—the same thing was played again and again.)

Perhaps I didn't enjoy mealtime because I hurried through it to get to the "good stuff."

Did their simple meals aid their ability to enjoy their family? Did they not overtire themselves by preparing a complicated dish?

Or, had they learned to give thanks and praise in tough times? Had God rewarded them by lifting their spirits?

I'm not pining for the "good old days" of dictatorial Romania, when an oppressive government whittled one's options to working, eating, and sleeping, but I am discovering we can learn from these women.

Perhaps we've become overloaded with options and

Help! The Ravenous Multitude Is after Me

hold such high expectations that disappointment is a certainty. As children, we learned that America is the land of opportunity where dreams come true. Is reality a letdown? Is the hard work that leads to the fulfillment of dreams sometimes looked at as an inconvenience—an interruption to our "happily ever after" promise we've expected since childhood?

No, a good mealtime is not synonymous with living in a country where oppression is the order of the day. But could it be that good things come by the effort and priority we give to them? Is mealtime any different? Treated as an afterthought or a necessary evil, doesn't it become a time of irritation and frustration?

Most of us don't go to great effort to obtain food. We have so much to choose from that our effort comes in keeping things simple and basic. We have the option of doing so many things at any given time of the day that our effort comes in defining the important things, then maintaining our priorities.

I'm reminded of the manna back in Moses' time. It was readily available and quickly prepared . . . a transitional food for a transitional time.

We, too, live in transitional times. As mothers, our families are growing and changing. We, too, need a manna. Simple food for busy times. Though it may not be classified as gourmet, served with helpings of love and pleasure, it will sustain and nourish.

When the children of Israel finally got through the wilderness, the Lord told them to save a jar of manna and store it in the ark of the covenant along with the Ten Commandments and Aaron's staff. The stored manna served as a reminder of *their need* and *God's provision* in the wilderness.

Who knows, someday when our children are grown and

Sock Hunting and Other Pursuits

gone, we might want to bronze a few carrot sticks or a tuna salad or even a box of Hamburger Helper as a reminder of "the good old days" when life was full—with children to care for and approximately 747 meals to prepare each year. Yes, *these* are the days. Let's enjoy them to the max.

TIME TO CONSIDER

1. How can we obtain the ability to enjoy mealtime or any kind of earthly pleasure (Eccles. 2:24, 25)? Think of a mealtime that was not set apart for any special reason, yet holds pleasant memories for you. What is it about these memories that makes them pleasant?

2. How can we find exceptional aspects in mundane happenings? List specific instances where an attitude or an outlook changed the course of feelings or events.

3. What happens to the gatherer (Eccles. 2:26)? How does this apply to working mothers?

4. Read Ecclesiastes 3:1-8. How can meal preparation also be a time to nurture as well as nourish your family?

5. What is God's gift to you according to Ecclesiastes 3:13? How can you practically apply this verse?

8

The Sock Hunt

As anyone who is old enough to wash clothes knows, washers and dryers not only *eat* socks—they *survive* on them. We humans erroneously believe that the appliances continue to work because we keep them oiled and clean the lint filter. We pay repairers big time bucks to tinker with them. However, if you'll observe a little more carefully, you'll probably notice that the need for repairing usually coincides with the absence of Jason's or Sarah's sock. We need to wake up and face the facts. These machines aren't broken—they merely have indigestion! How often does a repairman "fix" a washing machine or a dryer that stays fixed for any length of time?

When these machines sputter as if their life were slipping away, it would be more effective to call the school nurse and run some Pepto Bismol through the wash cycle than to call Sears.

Sock Hunting and Other Pursuits

Laundry is just one of the many tasks we face. We could refuse to do it, but we probably wouldn't like the results. (I can't think of anyone who actually *likes* dirty clothes or mildewed towels.) Some people pay others to do it. Sounds like a plan to me. However, my pocketbook and I don't see eye-to-eye on the subject—yet. As of now, either I or some other unfortunate member of my household does it. Sometimes I've felt guilty at my lack of enthusiasm over this weekly project, but I know many who share my distaste. Listen to what Toby Devens Schuartz says about laundry-day blues.

Dear Lord,

Thank you for nylon, rayon, Dacron and polyester.

Help me to remember as I approach this task I dislike how my mother boiled, starched and ironed my collars and ruffles.

Give me strength, please, to refrain from dumping colored with white. Lead my hand to measure detergent in its proper amount and add the fabric softener at the rinse cycle.

Keep me away from the telephone, television and coffee cup while the dryer is on—I have seen what overheating does to permanent press and, lo, I am afraid.

And, Lord, when I get to sorting, folding and stacking, guide me in the intricate origami of my husband's T-shirts—he asks for so little, only sleeves turned back and a sharp midline crease—and turn my heart toward the piping voice and sweet profile of my daugh-ter. Let me recall her as my delight, not as the only child on the block with six and a half pairs of underpants and twelve patterned socks, none of which match.

The Sock Hunt

Finally, dear Lord, lead me to look up from the dazzle of prints and stripes into Your sunlight which is infinitely brighter than any Dynamo wash and praise the beauty and good order of this world which renews itself constantly and, thankfully, without my help. Amen.[1]

In a household that includes children, an indeterminate number of tasks must get done, although no one enjoys doing them. Below is a list—which shocked me at first—of a few things parents spend their time on. I'm sure you can add some chores of your own.

vacuum	wash car
mop floor	change car oil
sweep floor	mow lawn
dust	fertilize yard
clean closets	spray for bugs
put dishes away	mend kids' clothes
grocery shop	put gas in car
carry groceries in	clean light fixtures
put groceries away	clean gutters
cook	weed yard
do dishes	prune trees
wipe down kitchen	water yard
clean bathroom	take kids to dentist
wash rugs	help kids with homework
take out garbage	change heat filter
wash windows	change vacuum filter
wash window sills	change filter in stove fan
pay bills	clip back bushes
do laundry	shop for kids' clothes
put laundry away	take kids to doctor
pick up dry cleaning	drive car pool

Sock Hunting and Other Pursuits

We'd probably all agree that "learning to get things done with the least fuss is not a gift but an acquired art."[2]

In their book *The Working Mother's Complete Handbook,* Gloria Norris and Jo Ann Miller write on the subject: "Tell yourself that no one but you is keeping score. Nowhere is it recorded that your hall closet is a disaster area, that there are thirteen unmatched socks in your son's bureau drawer, that at least two cap guns and one headless doll are lurking behind the couch cushions. Although we don't suggest that you blithely breeze off to the office letting the dishes and toys fall where they may, clinging to rigid standards of tidiness can only be self-destructive."[3]

I do my best to remember this each time I enter my son's room.

HOW TO MOTIVATE KIDS TO CLEAN THEIR ROOMS

After spending a few minutes tidying up his room, my son emerges. "I got it all cleaned up, Mom." When I check and see the debris still scattered across the carpet, I look directly into his eyes for a sign that he's joking. He's not. He is so sincere, he nearly convinces me that it *is* clean—even though I possess 20/20 vision. I've finally realized he isn't trying to lie, he merely sees the room differently than I do. What appears as a mess to me is really the skyscraper he and his friend Keith began last evening (out of Legos, Tinker Toys, and Lincoln Logs combined with a few Pick-up Sticks). Unfortunately, Keith's mother called him home before they could finish. It's a building in progress, and "we can't take it down, please."

I try to remember once again that "clinging to rigid standards of tidiness can only be self-destructive" as I venture down the hall to my daughters' room (which they share). Here I see a whole network of book bags, tennis

The Sock Hunt

shoes, and gum wrappers on the floor. But of course, depending on which daughter is home, it's *all* the other daughter's stuff.

I said, I try to remember; and some days I do pretty well. However, on those other days—when company is coming in twenty minutes—I'd like for my children to see what I see, but it doesn't happen. Standards of cleanliness differ from person to person, and mine are definitely different from theirs. But then again, they are more relaxed and certainly farther from an ulcer than I am. And their innocent eyes hold no hint of conspiracy—so I can only surmise that they aren't *trying* to indicate I'm a slovenly housekeeper. They just manage to do it anyway. It's almost forgivable.

Let's face it, when we're rushed and someone doesn't comprehend our request for help, it's frustrating. I've given up trying to motivate them to see what I see. It's not going to happen, at least not until they're thirtysomething and suddenly notice things like unmade beds and skates on the floor. At ages six to twelve we are only conscious that Mom is a grump.

I've resorted to using charts. Once a week, I escort my children to their rooms and close the door. On the back of each door is a checklist. It goes something like this:

1. Are all the drawers closed?
2. Is everything off the floor?
3. Is the closet door closed?
4. Is the bed made?
5. Is the dresser cleared off?
6. Do you love Mom?

I know it borders on abuse, but I don't allow them to come out until they've checked everything off the list. Interestingly enough, they've never eaten more than two meals in a row in there.

Sock Hunting and Other Pursuits

The above is just one tip that can help us organize our homes. However, to keep it that way will require not only our own efforts, but the ability to delegate chores to other family members. This isn't that easy. Dr. Magid outlines some challenges that arise as we attempt to organize our homes and lives.

PROBLEMS, SYMPTOMS, AND POSSIBLE SOLUTIONS

Problem:
Wasting time (spending time on low priority, unimportant things).

Self-Castigation for:
1. Talking too much on the phone.
2. Excessive unscheduled socializing with unexpected visitors.
3. Spending the last two hours waiting at the TV repair shop, auto mechanic's, and so on.
4. Spending the entire morning at the grocery store when you'd intended to stay only 45 minutes.

Possible solutions:
1. Don't be a slave to the phone or doorbell. Both were intended to be conveniences, not burdens. You can always:
    a. Buy an inexpensive answering machine for the phone and monitor your calls.
    b. Tell other family members you don't want to be disturbed and ask them to answer the phone or door and take messages.
    c. Request that friends and family generally call and visit you during specified times (in morning, after dinner, before 10:00 P.M.).
    d. Not answer phone or door.

The Sock Hunt

2. Teach or request other family members (especially children) to respect your need to be alone or work uninterrupted. A closed door can and should be respected at home as much as it is elsewhere.

3. Avoid "stream of consciousness" behavior in which you start one thing, which leads to another, which leads to another, which leads to another, and so on. Don't clean the sink and then decide you might as well reorganize the cupboards and, as long as you're doing that, mop the floor. Stick to your intentions.

4. Invest time and money in preventive car and appliance maintenance. The tire you get fixed now involves far less hassle than the tire you have to get repaired in New York City at 2:00 A.M.

5. Look around for stores that deliver dry cleaning, groceries, pharmaceuticals, and so on to your home and see whether the delivery charge is worth it.

6. Investigate the possibility of hiring (or trading services with) a neighborhood teenager, college student, or retiree to do your errand-hopping.

Problem:
Doing it all.

Symptoms:
Beliefs such as:
1. "No one can do this as well as I can, let alone better."
2. "I can't burden anyone else with these things, so I'll just have to do them myself."
3. "In the end, I'll get saddled with the task if I want it done, so I might as well do it from the start."

Possible solutions:
1. Ask yourself two questions:

Sock Hunting and Other Pursuits

   a. Does this task need to be done at all?
   b. Does this task need to be done the way I do it?

If the task doesn't need to be done, eliminate it. If the task needs to be done but doesn't have to be done your way, delegate it to someone else. If it does need to be done, and for some idiosyncratic reason it *must* be done your way, don't delegate that task. You'll end up criticizing the way the other person does it, or, even worse, doing it yourself.

2. Eliminate the supervisory role. Once tasks are delegated by mutual agreement, forget about those things you aren't responsible for.

3. Don't automatically assume a task because you're the only one who knows how to do it. People are trainable! Be patient and encouraging.[4]

HOW TO MOTIVATE KIDS TO HELP AT HOME

Everybody would like to have help around the house, but how does one get it?

1. Don't be vague! A simple "I'd like you all to help around the house more" won't cut it here. Children may genuinely want to help (probably not, though), but this statement doesn't give them a clue as to *how* to help.

   a. Make a list of specific tasks that they can do. This serves two purposes:

      1. It gives them hope. A list of tasks can be completed. After finishing everything on their list, they can be assured that you won't run after them all day to get more help.

      2. It gives them a sense of accomplishment. They've completed what you've asked them to do, so provide stars or red dots they can place beside a listed chore when completed.

   b. Reward your children for a job well done.

The Sock Hunt

1. Money. If you opt to use money as a reward, decide how much you'll pay them for the work, then divide that amount by the number of chores you ask them to complete during that time. This gives you an amount they will receive for each chore. Write that amount next to each task. Enter the total at the bottom of the chart.

2. Other. If you decide to do something other than pay your children for their work, then specify each week (in writing) an activity or other form of acknowledgement.

c. Pay promptly. In this respect, children are much like adults; if they are promised pay on Friday, and for some reason it doesn't come, they lose motivation.

2. If your children "forget" to do a chore, don't do it for them.

a. Let the child realize the consequences of forgetfulness. For example, if a child is supposed to take out the garbage, don't you do it instead. Take it only as far as the child's room. Or, if everyone agrees to make dinner one night a week and one child consistently "forgets" on a specified night, go out to eat and let that child find something at home.[5]

b. This won't always work. If your son is supposed to make his bed before going to school, and he doesn't, he's probably not going to feel too bad about seeing it unmade when he comes home. You have two choices:

1. Insist that he does it when he comes in.

2. Dock his pay and close the door. (Personally, I prefer this method. I'm a little more picky about the common areas like the living room, dining room, and kitchen, because they affect everyone.)

While this method won't have our children hopping out of bed saying "Yippee! I get to sweep and vacuum today!" at least they know specifically *how* we want them to help and how helping will benefit them.

Sock Hunting and Other Pursuits

This method has worked well at our house. I used to spend my day off and much of my evenings performing household chores. Now, my three children have three tasks apiece in the morning and spend fifteen or twenty minutes doing them. That's nine chores I *don't* do and time shaved off my daily schedule. That leaves several hours a week (they don't do chores on the weekend) to take them to the park or some other activity we all enjoy.

Be prepared, though. Kids don't automatically perform these household pastimes exactly the way we would. This method requires turning a blind eye to the slight ring around the tub that you'd see if you were to look closely and enjoying the fresh smell instead. The little bit of Comet that didn't get rinsed out in the corner will ensure you that they are trying . . . and learning. Not a bad combination—trying and learning. Kind of sounds like the stuff life is make of. And this isn't a bad life. In fact it can be quite pleasant sometimes.

Like on those rare occasions when we pull the socks from the dryer, and (wonder of wonders) they match.

TIME TO CONSIDER

1. Identify any chores you're doing that could just as easily be done by one of your children. How can you "make the most of every opportunity" (Eph. 5:15) and, at the same time, teach your children how to take more responsibility for themselves?

2. Identify your particular time-wasters. How can you eliminate them?

3. Have you prayed about household priorities? What is God saying to you is most important at the present time?

The Sock Hunt

4. What are some ways you can simplify your life? What can you throw out? Stop doing? Spend less energy on so you can spend your time on what's important?

9

Everyone Wants Something from Me

First Daughter: "Mom, where's my blue shirt?"
Son: "Mom, can Chaz come over tonight?"
Second Daughter: "Mom, will you pick me up from Camp Fire at 5:30?"
Husband: "Honey, you can run me to the airport later this morning, can't you?"
Friend: "Will you stop by and get in on at least a little of my Tupperware party?"
Boss: "I'll need these from you by three o'clock."
Sales Clerk: "Just fill in your name and address. . . "
Car Mechanic: "That'll be three hundred dollars."
Doctor: "When you're finished, just put the little cup inside the window—okay?"

As WMs do we ever "get finished"? Have you ever promised that when you "get finished," you'll slow down, relax, and do some healthy things for your mind, body,

Sock Hunting and Other Pursuits

and spirit—only to have time slip by and the cycle begin all over again?

You know you need refreshment when life becomes so frenzied that you get up one morning, spray your underarms with Pine-Sol and your hair with tile cleaner, coating both with a foamy white layer. We do things like this because we are distracted. But is it any wonder? *Remembering* some of our schedules, let alone pulling them off, puts a drain on our faculties.

That's why it's so important to schedule light-hearted activities. Things like playing with our children, engaging in a hobby, or taking a walk recharge us.

We sometimes lose touch with our need for recharging. For instance, my battery-operated lap-top word processor works as well five minutes before the juice is gone as it does when it's fully charged. Then, right before the power ceases, it begins to beep every thirty seconds. It does this a few times and is gone. If I'm engrossed in my work, I may recognize the beep, but assure myself that I've got another minute or so before the screen goes blank. I may choose to ignore the signal. If I'm really enmeshed in what I'm doing, I may not even *hear* the signal. Then I lose hours worth of work in a machine that "suddenly" goes dead.

We may not *feel* a need to recharge. After all, we're busy right now. However, if we continue to put off times of refreshment, it's only inevitable that the screen of our mind will eventually go blank or become distorted. We must somehow recognize our limitations and convey the message effectively to others.

We all know that children often push things to the limit—just to learn where the boundaries are. Sometimes they go too far. Sometimes we go too far. However, we don't usually do it for the same reasons.

We do it because those around us have needs and we are

Everyone Wants Something from Me

capable of meeting those needs. It just takes a little time. And when we don't have the time? We try to do it anyway. A few days ago, I observed something in nature that reminded me of this phenomena.

THE MOTHER DUCK

A mother duck and her seven ducklings all swam close to the river's shoreline where I sat. Suddenly, all of the ducklings began to swim at her at once. As she struggled to stay afloat, a fisherman beside me said, "I hope they don't drown her."

She continued her efforts for a few moments. Then, when it appeared that she might sink, she spread her wings wide, right into the midst of them. The ducklings quickly scattered. They gathered into a formation off to the side of her; close enough for protection, but far enough away not to threaten her survival.

Is it possible to stay open and receptive to others, yet leave enough room so that *we* can maneuver? When we sink into irritability or depression because we feel overwhelmed, our children become the beneficiaries of our pain, disappointment, and/or self-rejection. ("I can't do everything for everybody, so something must be wrong with me.") We then project our pain and self-rejection onto our children.

Sure, it's good to rely on God and place our faith in his word. The Bible says, "With God all things are possible" (Matt. 19:26) and "I can do everything through him [Christ] who gives me strength" (Phil. 4:13). However, when everything comes at us at once, we're not suddenly transformed into the Christian version of Dyna-Woman simply by reciting these verses. Instead, we are given a brain; we are given a heart. God speaks to both and he guides us.

When her ducklings lunged at her, the mother duck

Sock Hunting and Other Pursuits

spread her wings in order to survive. Although the ducklings remained close, they scattered far enough away so that she could stay afloat.

We are responsible to provide the space we need for our own emotional and physical survival. Through prayer God helps us with this, providing both rest and strength. However, he leaves much of the responsibility to us.

Remember the story of Nehemiah, the one commissioned to rebuild the walls of Jerusalem? The walls lay in ruins because the Israelites had been exiled from their homeland. Nehemiah gained favor with the king and was commissioned to rebuild these walls of protection around the city.

People weren't happy about this and came to Nehemiah, trying to distract him from his task. However, Nehemiah had a purpose, and he was *not* going to be distracted. He built the wall.

God knew that these people were coming. He could have circumvented them—causing a donkey jam on the road to Damascus or something, affecting the highway system in the whole area, enabling Nehemiah to go about his business without thinking about priorities. But he left Nehemiah to deal with the situation. While most of our families and friends wouldn't purposely throw us off course, in trying to get their needs met, it happens.

How did Nehemiah handle it? He didn't try to appease people.

WHAT IS APPEASEMENT, ANYWAY?

Are we appeasing when we take the kids to the park for no other reason than enjoyment? No, that's not appeasement, that's play. And we need plenty of it. Appeasement is when we say, "Sure, I'll be a table hostess at the next monthly tea" because we know the chairperson needs us, when we actually had no intention of even attending. We had planned to take the kids bowling that night.

While we are responsible to love and nurture our children, we are not responsible to appease them. Recognizing the difference for this inequality can mean the variance between actively loving our families and merely existing on an appeasement level.

Jesus was all too aware of this when he said, "If someone forces you to go one mile, go with him two miles" (Matt. 5:41).

The first mile is duty; the second mile is love.

WHO HAS TIME FOR THE SECOND MILE?

Second mile travel is possible only when we become choosy about our activities—when our lives are streamlined in simplicity. How do we do this? We can refuse to merely appease, and choose rather to love. Appeasement is a *reaction*. Love, on the other hand, is an *action*.

We can liken an appeaser to a Ping-Pong ball: tap its surface and it sails across the room in whatever direction it's propelled—externally.

On the other hand, our lives can be led in the spirit of love, propelled inwardly. We're anchored to a rock, and if we move, we move with purpose.

As moms, we respond to life around us. The baby needs his diaper changed. We may not have planned on doing it at that time, but we do it. A child becomes ill, we stay home to nurse him. We respond to genuine urgency.

Appeasement is: "Mom, will you pick me up from track practice today? Dad always comes and get me in the VW Bug. It's sooo embarrassing!"

If it's inconvenient for me to pick her up because of my work schedule or other prior plans, and it will throw me off course, forcing me to double up my work load or go to

Sock Hunting and Other Pursuits

bed later to catch up, she *will* get over riding in a pea green VW Bug. Yes, it will be tough (it *is* an ugly car—some very large individuals jumped on its top so it's not rounded like it should be). However, it may increase her compassion for any other child who is forced to ride around in a squashed car that looks like someone blew his nose on it.

Appeasement doesn't build a child in the long run. I've seen moms spend copious amounts of time trying to make a kid happy. Yet the kid is seldom happy.

On the other hand, when we see all the "cooperation" another child receives from a parent (who brings the spelling book or forgotten lunch to school), we may wonder if we're neglectful. Are we being insensitive to their needs or simply allowing them to feel the effects of real life on this planet—the kind of life that seldom sends us on our way in a shiny new Jaguar?

THE WISDOM OF FLEXIBILITY

A working mother's days aren't often destined to go strictly according to plan. When my children were smaller and unexpected happenings more common, I often felt discouraged when I looked at my list of eighty-nine things to do and found I had only accomplished three of them. However, if I can see that what I did that day was indeed worthwhile, that I accomplished one or two things I believed in (no, I didn't clean the garage, but I *did* comfort my daughter's hurt feelings), I can congratulate myself on a job well done.

I recently discussed appeasement, accomplishment, and planning with marriage and family therapist Dennis Chamberlin.

How would you define appeasement?

Chamberlin: Appeasement is to comply to the needs of a system rather than to consciously attempt balance. It's to act on impulse rather than on planned, thought-out strategy. I liken it to a zoo keeper throwing food to animals in a zoo—whomever makes the most noise gets theirs first. His actions fulfill the needs of the moment but make little difference in the overall structure of the system.

What are the dangers of this type of behavior?

Chamberlin: The number one danger is that it often skirts the real issues. A person will always act out values and move toward goals, if not in an intentional manner, then haphazardly. The process will be controlled by circumstance.

What do you see as the greatest need for a working mother in this area?

Chamberlin: A need for clarity. A working mother either acts as two people operating in two different systems, or she finds a way to balance and be effective in both. Clarity is taking all the different aspects of herself, her family, and her surroundings and, like a mix of ingredients, creating a balanced recipe and baking a cake.

That sounds good, but how do we do this?

Chamberlin: By spending time clarifying priorities, goals, needs, and resources. By writing these down, you can refer to them in order to determine if your involvements are in line with your basic principles.

You've mentioned goals, needs, and resources. Could you elaborate on how we can clarify each of these issues?

Chamberlin: In the area of goals, it's important to ask, "What do I want to achieve? What am I aiming for? Are my present habits likely to accomplish these goals?" By taking the time for self-reflection, a woman can get a picture and determine if this is the direction she wishes to continue in. Doing this prevents her from fooling herself—concluding that just because she keeps moving, she is actually going somewhere. Unchanneled, constant mo-

Sock Hunting and Other Pursuits

tion not only leads to stress, but to burnout as well. That's why it's so crucial that a working mother carefully consider the other two factors I mentioned (needs and resources). To be realistic, our goals must include these considerations.

1. *Needs:* This category is necessarily distinct. A working mother is operating in a family system, unique in its makeup of individuals. The needs of her spouse and children as well as her personal necessities must be considered in the overall development of goals and values.

2. *Resources:* The time, energy, and support (personal and emotional as well as structural support) available to her. Much forethought is of great value in this area. This reality often determines not only what is possible but what is wise to endeavor.

Unresolved conflicts, unforgiven sin, unfulfilled longings, unresolved anger, unhealed wounds: these all put a drain on resources and can result in loss of energy and exhaustion.

You mentioned burnout *earlier. We hear a lot about burnout, but what is its technical meaning?*

Chamberlin: A syndrome that involves a certain pattern encompassing the physical, social, and emotional areas of life. There are several degrees to the burnout process, ranging from mild bouts of irritation and a general sense of frustration, to the severe: clear physical symptoms and ailments, including back pain, ulcer, etc. This process involves a loss of idealism, energy, and purpose combined with a general sense of fatigue. Herbert Froidenberger defined it: to fail, to wear out, or to become exhausted by excessive demands on energy, strength, and resources. Characterized by: lack of enthusiasm, sense of stagnation, general sense of frustration, futility, and apathy. There is a pattern to these:

Everyone Wants Something from Me

- Enthusiasm—high hopes, unrealistic expectations
- Stagnation—doesn't replace all in life
- Frustration—questions job and the worth of personal goals
- Apathy—exists, tries to meet minimum requirement, no frustration or fuel left, is without feeling

While these are symptoms and patterns of burnout, they are not exclusive to burnout. They could be the results of other factors, including:

- Serious physical illness
- Biochemical reaction to medication or a depression disorder
- Poor nutrition and lack of exercise
- Traumatic events in the past or present

We don't suddenly one day wake up and observe, "I'm burned-out." What leads to burnout?

Chamberlin: Several things. First, too much work and too little play. Second, a neurotic need for self-verification that is met by one's work. Third, inadequate intake for the amount of output: a rigid, graceless system. Under this category is the Christian without an accurate and healthy concept of grace. God's grace is personal, forgiving, and accepting; and if it is missing, one has no way to gain inward refreshment.

You used the word stress *earlier. Is this the same thing as burnout?*

Chamberlin: No, these words are not interchangeable. Burnout differs from stress in that if you were to take even a constantly stressed individual out of the stressful situation, the symptoms would disappear. A person experiencing burnout, however, possesses many internal aspects. A burned-out individual needs an appropriate time of healing and restoration.[1]

HEALING AND RESTORATION

Part of healing is learning how to deal more effectively in our surroundings and how to communicate our needs to others. We need to incorporate new procedures to help us cope. Haphazardly dealing with situations as they arise may not be the most productive means of developing ourselves, our families, or our spirituality. Rather, a clear understanding of values and goals is essential to begin to function in a manner "worthy of our calling" (Eph. 4:1 KJV).

In the workplace, meetings are held for the express purpose of airing differences and solving problems. During these times, we distance ourselves from the tasks at hand and come together to communicate with one another. Families need this type of communication, or "family council," in non-crisis times. Here, strategy can be developed rationally, without the intense emotional responses to momentary, emergency attempts at "working it out" in a crisis.

The other crucial aspect of healing and restoration is the clear understanding of God's grace that Chamberlin mentioned. There is a healing that happens in the natural sense by simply recognizing and caring for an injury. But beyond that, healing and restoration come from deep within our being, from a private place God alone can touch. We may grow weary and lack heart for some of the more repetitive tasks we do each day. In our weariness, we often say and do things we later wish we hadn't, yet God doesn't react to us in anger.

Instead, he comes to us with arms outstretched and compassion reflected in his beautiful eyes. After enveloping us in his embrace and allowing us to cry for a bit, he holds out a gift. He says, "I brought something especially for you. I want you to have this because I love and value you so much. You are precious to me."

Everyone Wants Something from Me

As you dry your tears, you untie the silk ribbons and remove the satin covering. You discover a small scroll surrounded by a beautiful piece of purple velvet. The parchment scroll is rolled, and a signet ring adorned with the seal of an alabaster dove holds it together. As you take the ring from the scroll, the gentle voice says, "Please wear the ring as a symbol of our union." You slip it on your finger and find it's the perfect size. The tender voice continues, "Please read the scroll. I inscribed the message just for you." You open the scroll and see that the beautiful script is written in crimson, as if it were penned in blood. It speaks to you of life. "I will give you a new heart and put a new spirit in you; I will remove from you your heart of stone and give you a heart of flesh."[2] When you look up from your reading, he is gone. But the ring, with its alabaster dove, remains on your finger, and the scroll is still in your hand.

While God occasionally grants us instantaneous healing through a dream, vision, or miracle, inner healing usually isn't immediate. He tells us: "They that *wait* upon the Lord shall renew their strength; they shall mount up with wings as eagles; they shall run, and not be weary; and they shall walk and not faint" (Isa. 40:31 KJV, italics added).

Notice the word *wait*. Healing often takes time. However, God isn't mad at you during this time. No, instead, the Holy Spirit is deep within your being, searching out the recesses of your soul. He knows your cares and your pain, and he weeps with you. He prays to his Father that you may experience restoration.

Earlier, we asked, "Who doesn't want something from me?" There is one who only wants to *give* you something—peace. That one is Jesus. And he waits for you, because he "longs to be gracious to you" (Isa. 30:18).

Sock Hunting and Other Pursuits

TIME TO CONSIDER

1. When everyone wants a piece of you, what are some practical things you can do to pull away with the Lord and renew your mind?

2. What are the benefits listed in the following verses of spending time with God (Ps. 91:1; 103:5-7)? What exactly does "spending time with God" mean? (Ps. 119:15; 145:5; Prov. 15:8; Mark 11:24)?

3. How can time spent doing mundane activities also be turned into time spent with God (Ps. 146:1)?

4. Are there areas of your life where you still feel that distance? Have you put "off limits" signs on any part of your being? If so, list those areas that you may be aware of.

5. Suppressed feelings put distance between people. Do you think we try so hard to be "good" that when we have a negative thought or feeling about God, we bury it and put distance between God and us? If so, what action can you take to close that distance so that God can be a loving father to you (Ps. 51:6; John 8:32)?

6. God does not expect us to go through this life without emotions. In fact, he made us with the ability to feel. Is it difficult for you to tell God how you honestly feel? Why or why not?

10

Is Love Possible on a Tight Schedule?

I recently heard two working moms discussing relationships. When one posed the question, "Is love possible on a tight schedule?" the other mom laughed.

"That's a good question," she said. And it is.

Given the business of combining work and home, along with the fact that the average length of a marriage in the United States is only about seven years, it seems many couples have answered no.

When pressing demands of others and the pull of time commitments compete with intimacy, marriage sometimes ceases to be a comfort and becomes, instead, like an infected boil which causes much pain until finally, one partner or the other seeks relief. At this point, many marriages end.

Daphne Rose Kingma, in her book *True Love . . . How to Make Your Relationship Sweeter, Deeper and More Passionate*, explains why.

Sock Hunting and Other Pursuits

We often think, at least unconsciously, that when we finally fall in love and decide to share our lives with another person, everything in our lives will fall into place. We'll "settle down," as we say, and, the implication is, we'll stay settled until "death do us part."

I call this the Shoe Box Notion of love. In this view, a relationship is like a shoe box or some other rather small container in which you keep something precious like your wedding bouquet. You wrap the flowers in tissue paper, put them in the box, put on the lid, place the box on the shelf, and hope the contents will stay just as they are forever and a day.

Unfortunately, this is precisely how many of us think about relationships. We put our love in a shoe box, stash it, and imagine we can retrieve it unchanged anytime we want. *We think we don't have to do anything to make sure it doesn't get moldy or moth-eaten.*[1]

Everyday marriages fall apart, not because the partners committed some great sin, but because they erroneously believed people don't change. But we do. We grow. It's crucial for the relationship to develop along with the individuals. When it fails to do so, it becomes irrelevant.

We foster this growth in our relationship when we allow our partner to mature and develop. "To do so, is always to be open to becoming much more than you were. To resist is to diminish yourself, to become, in the end, much less than you could be."[2]

The "shoe box notion" of love resists change, ignores growth, and eventually stifles both individuals. Time is a crucial factor in this pattern. When we are overextended, we don't have time to adjust to anything new. An overextended person often feels the need to keep some things

Is Love Possible on a Tight Schedule?

just as they are. They're easier to deal with that way.

Time management expert Dr. Diana Scharf Hunt recently said, "People must understand that time affects everything we do: How we feel about a particular activity—be it pleasure or work—is often determined by the amount of time we have to do it in. The less time we have, the more pressured—and negative—we feel."[3]

Ask yourself this question: How much time do I allot for showing love to my mate? The intent of this question isn't to induce guilt, but rather to enable us to determine if we are accomplishing what we'd like to in this area. Marriage requires more than the leftovers of our time. If that's all we're prepared to offer it, the outlook is less than promising.

The writer of Proverbs summed up this need to consciously be a seeker of time in relationships when he said, "Those who plan good find love and faithfulness. All hard work brings a profit, but mere talk leads only to poverty" (Prov. 14:22, 23).

What these two verses tell me in terms of relationship is that it will take the hard work of *planning* if I'm going to be rich in the area of love. However, on a WM's busy schedule, that can be tricky.

Sally Wendkos Olds, author of *Working Parents' Survival Guide*, gives some terrific clues on making a place and time in your life for making love.

> Put a lock on your bedroom door. Nothing dampens ardor so effectively as the knowledge that a pajama-clad cherub could wander in at any time.
>
> Create an attractive setting in your bedroom. Is it neat and inviting, or is it the depository of all the clutter you're embarrassed to leave around the rest of the house? It would be better to have a neighborhood reputation as a sloppy housekeeper than for you and

Sock Hunting and Other Pursuits

your spouse to have to slog through piles of laundry and old newspapers in order to reach the bed.

If you're always too tired at night, set the alarm for an hour earlier than you usually get up. Funny how waking up at 5:00 A.M. is much more inviting when the object is lovemaking.

If one of you is an "owl" who likes to stay up late and the other a "lark" who is energetic early in the day, take turns accommodating to each other's schedules. The "lark" can take an early evening nap to stay up later, for example.

If your children have begun to go to sleep later than you do, don't wait. There is nothing wrong with telling the children that you and your spouse are going into your bedroom and that you don't want to be disturbed. This is the *best* kind of sex education—letting them know that the two of you are interested in each other. You can even ask them to answer the telephone and to tell callers you're busy and will phone back the next day. (Chances are, if they're staying up so late, they're the ones getting the calls, anyway.)

Think "Why not?" when your partner expresses interest in making love, even if you're not in the mood. If you set aside the time for sex and concentrate on pleasing your partner, you'll often be pleasantly surprised to find that before you realize it, you are in the mood.

Occasionally telephone each other during the day with a sexual invitation. A throaty voice promising splendid pleasure later on arouses a mouth-drying sensation of anticipation even among long-married couples.

Plan ahead. As the Zussmans wrote in their book *Getting Together,* "Look, you plan everything else in life. You plan your ski weekends, even though you don't know whether or not it's going to snow. You schedule going to church services on Sunday. . . . As for getting in the mood, the key usually lies in arousing your expectations. The best way to put yourself in the mood is to make a date." Couples who have followed this advice have found that it can result in some of the most memorable times of their lives.[4]

COMING TOGETHER EMOTIONALLY AND SPIRITUALLY

While it is a challenge to find time together physically, there are times (like when we've been going in different directions all day) when coming together on an emotional and spiritual level can be even more difficult. Part of the reason for this is what psychologists call "transition time." Work and love require such different aspects of ourselves. Work is image; love is minus the pretense—being known as we are. Work is hustle; love is tranquil. Work is fulfilling requirements; love is giving. Work is duty; love is free.

TRANSITION TIMES

Is it any wonder that it may take a bit of time to switch from one mode to the other? We "transition" from work to home several ways: reading the paper, spending a few minutes alone, taking a walk, listening to music, taking a bath, driving, etc.

Although these transitions are necessary, problems can develop in the areas of timing and a couple's understanding of one another.

The woman who has worked at a desk all day may want to come home and do something active, such as take a walk or ride a bike. However, if her husband has spent his day loading trucks, he may be physically spent and want

Sock Hunting and Other Pursuits

only to watch TV and eat. Sometimes it takes one person longer than the other to switch the focus from work to home. It's so easy to take these differences personally, when in fact, both persons may be doing their best.

I grew up in a home where my father worked with machinery. When he arrived home, he took a ten-minute shower and then went to the kitchen, ready to talk. My husband, on the other hand, works with people all day. He talks and negotiates. It takes him longer to unwind and feel up to conversation. Although I, too, work with people, I also travel in my job. During the hour it takes me to drive home, I listen to relaxing music and stop for something cool to drink. By the time I arrive home, I'm ready to communicate.

It has taken me some time to realize that my husband isn't trying to annoy or avoid me when we arrive home at the same time, and he's uncommunicative—perhaps he merely needs that time for transition. He hasn't had the hour's drive that I have.

You may have small children who are unable to occupy themselves for the time it takes you to unwind. If your job is so close to home that you don't have time to relax in the car, it may be wise to stop on your way home from work and read, walk, or drink a cup of herbal tea. Many parents feel guilty about doing this because they've been gone from the children all day. However, seeing them twenty minutes later isn't nearly as harmful as being a grouch because you didn't allow yourself the time to relax and feel pleasant.

In *Balancing Work and Home*, Vicky Warren writes about that time when we *do* begin to communicate.

1. Communication is key. Don't expect him to read your mind! If you have a need, let him know. Risk vulnerability.

Is Love Possible on a Tight Schedule?

2. See him as your teammate—not your adversary. You're in this together. Encourage one another. Seeing the strength of the bond between Mom and Dad will instill a feeling of security in your child(ren).

3. Let him know that you respect him. A husband often feels guilty when his wife returns to work. Sarcastic remarks that undermine his authority and leadership in the home will only heighten this feeling and make him feel "inadequate" as a provider.

4. Pray with and for each other. This will bind your hearts together.

5. Demonstrate a Philippians 2 attitude and practice 1 Corinthians 13 love towards one another.[5]

If we had only these areas to concentrate on after work, it might be a breeze. However, we may have tired and cranky children, a hungry family, a house that hardly looks like you stayed home and cleaned all day. It's not like all we've got to do is share our deep inner selves with each other at the end of the day. Instead, communication is often centered on who will do laundry and who will fix dinner. Instead of the sweet, loving words we may have anticipated hearing and speaking, we may, at times, find ourselves barking at each other.

Don Dinkmeyer and Jon Carlson recognized this in *Time for a Better Marriage* when they talked of sprinkling our mundane household conversations with phrases that focus on the positive:

"I like . . ."
"I appreciate . . ."
"I enjoyed . . ."
"I value . . ."
"I respect . . ."[6]

Let's face it, as couples with children, many of the

Sock Hunting and Other Pursuits

things we talk about, by necessity, are not very exciting. We *care* that the garbage got taken out, but the knowledge probably won't *thrill* us. Our husbands may *care* that we vacuumed the floor, but the knowledge won't *thrill* them. One way to take the boredom out of such talk is by using both eye contact and touch. Both are essential for exciting communication.

I do some fragrance modeling for department stores now and then. The first thing they taught me about applying fragrance was to gently hold the person's wrist after spraying the scent. This is for two reasons: one, because right after a fragrance is sprayed, there is a strong alcohol smell. After a few moments, it dissipates and the actual scent can be detected. The other reason is that human beings respond to touch. The wrist is held while we make eye contact with the customer and tell them a little about the ingredients in the scent and the history behind it. Some fragrance companies believe so strongly in the power of touch that they no longer demonstrate the spray form of the scent. Instead, they offer the cream or lotion, which is gently massaged into the customer's hand.

Cosmetic companies pay people to stand out in the middle of a department store aisle, merely because they know the power of touch and eye contact. They do it to make money.

These same principles work at home. Sure, household talk can be a bore, but try it with eye contact and touch. If our relationships have lost some sizzle, it's important that we try. Morals aren't what they used to be in this world. If we aren't endeavoring to put some excitement into our relationships, you can bet a woman out there somewhere may want to give it a try. In the '90s, sexual temptation is almost overwhelming. Twenty years ago, few women would openly pursue a married man. Today, much of the

Is Love Possible on a Tight Schedule?

shame has disappeared from the world's point of view, and everyone is fair game. A man no longer needs to go out of his way to find temptation. Chances are it will find him. Divorce statistics among Christians bear this out: they're *not* significantly different than those of non-Christians.

Most of these sad statistics don't begin with a night of wild, passionate sex. They begin, perhaps at the office, with lingering eye contact and a soft brush of the hand. Yet if these needs are fulfilled at home, your husband will be better equipped to withstand temptation.

Sandwiching our household tidbits between two affirmative statements along with eye contact and touch is in essence what Paul said in Philippians. "Finally brothers, whatever is true, whatever is noble, whatever is right, whatever is pure, whatever is lovely, whatever is admirable—if anything is excellent or praiseworthy—think about such things. . . . And the God of peace will be with you" (Phil. 4:8, 9).

Where there is peace, love has an opportunity to grow. It is in this growth process that we will determine for ourselves the answer to the question posed at the beginning of this chapter: *Is love possible on a tight schedule?*

We decide the answer. Are we willing to plan for love? Are we willing to be flexible about transition methods and timing? Are we willing to go to the extra effort to communicate in the method of Philippians 4:8, 9?

If we are willing, the opportunity is there.

> If I speak in the tongues
> of men and of angels,
> but have not love,
> I am only a resounding gong
> or a clanging cymbal.

Sock Hunting and Other Pursuits

> If I have the gift of prophecy
> and can fathom all mysteries
> and all knowledge,
> and if I have a faith
> that can move mountains,
> but have not love,
> I am nothing.
>
> If I give all I possess to the poor
> and surrender my body to flames,
> but have not love,
> I gain nothing.
>
> 1 Corinthians 13:1-3

TIME TO CONSIDER

1. How can Proverbs 14:22 assist you in building a rewarding relationship with your husband?

2. What does Proverbs 14:23 tell you about "lip service"? How can we apply this philosophy to our marriage relationship? To our relationship with our children?

3. What do you feel your marriage is in need of most? What would you like to see happen? What have you done in the past twenty-four hours to meet that same need for your husband?

4. How important is love in your life? Is it important enough to you to *do* anything about it? To show you care? According to 1 Corinthians 13:2, what are we if we have no love? What steps can you take to *show* love to your husband this week?

Is Love Possible on a Tight Schedule?

5. It's so easy to allow our busyness to crowd out loving feelings. Has that happened to you? To your husband? What can you do to promote those good feelings once again?

Source Notes

INTRODUCTION

1. Cheryl Russell, *100 Predictions for the Baby Boom* (New York: Plenum Press, 1987), p. 156.

CHAPTER 1

1. Kay Kuzma, *Working Mothers* (Los Angeles: Stratford Press, 1981), p. xi-xii.
2. Kuzma, *Working Mothers,* p. xii.
3. *Information Please Almanac 1990,* 43rd ed. (Boston: Houghton Mifflin Co., 1990), p. 61.
4. *Information Please Almanac 1990,* 43rd ed., p. 61.
5. Kuzma, *Working Mothers,* p. xii.
6. Vicky Warren, "Balancing Work and Home," *Christian Psychology For Today,* Spring 1989, p. 3.
7. Mike Yorkey, "Motherhood in the '90s," *Focus on the Family,* January 1990, p. 3.

8. "Motherhood in the '90s," p. 2.

9. "Balancing Work and Home," p. 4.

10. Elsa Houtz, *The Working Mother's Guide to Sanity* (Eugene, OR: Harvest House Publishers, 1989), p. 106.

11. "Balancing Work and Home," p. 4.

12. Jodi Detrick, unpublished manuscript. Used by permission of author.

CHAPTER 2

1. Media Mark Research Inc., (New York: Spring 1990 study).

2. Jean Bethke Elstain, quoting Shulamith Firestone, "Feminists Against the Family," *The Nation*, 17 November 1979, p. 498.

3. Betty Friedan, *Second Stage* (New York: Summit Books, 1981), p. 34.

4. Arlene Rossen Cardozo, *Sequencing* (New York: Atheneum 1986), p. 72.

5. Information Please Almanac 1990, 43rd ed. (Boston: Houghton Mifflin Co., 1990), p. 61.

6. Sue Campbell, "What's a Mommy War?" *Special Report: Family,* August-October 1990, p. 14.

7. Rose Kennedy, "Why Are We so Black and White?" *Special Report: Family*, August-October 1990, p. 21.

8. 1 Cor. 4:5.

9. Drs. Robert Hemfelt, Frank Minirth, and Paul Meier, *We Are Driven* (Nashville: Thomas Nelson Publishers, 1991), p. 163.

10. Hemfelt, Minirth, and Meier, *We Are Driven,* p. 164.

11. Catherine Mercier, unpublished maunscript. Used by permission of author.

Source Notes

CHAPTER 3

1. John Henry Jowett, *Come Ye Apart* (New York: Fleming H. Revell Company, 1920), p. 204.
2. Jowett, *Come Ye Apart*, p. 204.
3. Jowett, *Come Ye Apart*, p. 204.
4. Patricia Rushford, personal interview with author, Turner, OR, August 1990.
5. Anita Shreeve, *Remaking Motherhood* (New York: Viking, 1987), p. 137.
6. Shreeve, *Remaking Motherhood*, p. 134.
7. Shreeve, *Remaking Motherhood*, p. 134.
8. Jowett, *Come Ye Apart*, p. 203.

CHAPTER 4

1. Patricia Rushford, *What Kids Need Most in a Mom* (Old Tappan, NJ: Fleming H. Revell Company, 1986), pp. 94, 95.

CHAPTER 5

1. Nancy Samalin, "Why Do I Always Feel Guilty?" *Ladies' Home Journal*, February 1988, p. 171.
2. Houtz, *The Working Mothers' Guide to Sanity*, p. 103.
3. Charles Swindoll, *Come Before Winter* (Wheaton, IL: Tyndale House Publishers, Inc., 1988), p. 27.
4. Swindoll, *Come Before Winter*, p. 27.

CHAPTER 6

1. Dr. Deborah Belle, "Attention Working Women . . . Rate Your Stress Life," *Redbook*, June 1990, p. 84.
2. Dr. Renee Y. Magid, *When Mothers and Fathers Work* (New York: AMACOM, 1987), p. 113.

Sock Hunting and Other Pursuits

3. Eleanor Berman, *Re-entering* (New York: Crown Publishers, 1980), p. 142.

4. Magid, *When Mothers and Fathers Work,* p. 127.

CHAPTER 7

1. A liberal paraphrase of Exodus 16.

2. Linda Moxley, *I Used to Be a Nice Person*, unpublished manuscrupt. Used by permission of the author.

3. Emilie Barns, *More Hours in My Day* (Eugene, OR: Harvest House Publishers, 1982), p. 123.

4. James T. Duke, "Wives' Employment Status and Marital Happiness of Religious Couples," *Review of Religious Research*, March 1988, p. 267.

5. "Balancing Work and Home," p. 4.

CHAPTER 8

1. Toby Devens Schuartz, *Mercy Lord, My Husband's in the Kitchen: and Other Equal Opportunity Conversations with God* (Garden City, NY: Doubleday & Co., Inc., 1981), p. 49.

2. Ann Russell and Patricia Fitzgibbons, *Career and Conflict* (Englewood Cliffs, NJ: Prentice Hall, 1982), p. 77.

3. Gloria Norris and Jo Ann Miller, *Working Mother's Complete Handbook* (New York: E.P. Dutton, 1979), p. 81.

4. Magid, *When Mothers and Fathers Work,* p. 42.

5. Sally Wendkos Olds, *Working Parents' Survival Guide* (Rocklin, CA: Prima Publishing and Communications, 1989), pp. 355, 356.

Source Notes

CHAPTER 9

1. Dennis Chamberlin, personal interview, Milwaukie, OR, April 1991.
2. Ezek. 36:26.

CHAPTER 10

1. Daphne Rose Kingma, *True Love . . . How to Make Your Relationship Sweeter, Deeper, and More Passionate* (Berkeley: Conari Press, 1991), pp. 6, 7.
2. Kingma, *True Love,* p. 7.
3. Pam Hait, "How to Make Time for Love," *Ladies' Home Journal,* February 1988, p. 69.
4. Olds, *Working Parents' Survival Guide*, p. 266.
5. "Balancing Work and Home," p. 5.
6. Don Dinkmeyer and Jon Carlson, *Time For A Better Marriage* (Circle Pines, MN: American Guidance Service, 1984), p. 74.

Support Groups– Places of Growth and Healing

Women are hungry for teaching and nurturing as they grapple with issues that touch them where they live—loss, self-worth, singleness, remarriage, and numerous other felt needs.

God's heart is to heal and restore his people. In fact, Jesus states this clearly in Luke 4:18, 19 when he announces that God has called him to minister to the oppressed, the hurting, and the brokenhearted. We read throughout the entire New Testament how he wants to equip the Body of Christ to join him in reaching out in love and support of the bruised and wounded. Support groups provide this special place where healing can happen—where women are given time and space to be open about themselves in the context of loving acceptance and honest caring.

WHAT IS A SUPPORT GROUP?

- A support group is a small-group setting which offers women a "safe place." The recommended size is from eight to ten people.
- It is a compassionate, nonthreatening, confidential place where women can be open about their struggles and receive caring and support in a biblically-based, Christ-centered atmosphere.
- It is an accepting place, where women are listened to and loved right where they are.
- It is a place where love and truth are shared and the Holy Spirit is present to bring God's healing.
- It is a place where women learn to take responsibility for making Christ-like choices in their own lives.
- A support group has designated leadership. Coleaders are strongly recommended to share the role of facilitators.
- It is a cohesive and consistent group. This implies "closing" it to additional participants after the second or third meeting before beginning with a new topic and group.

WHAT SUPPORT GROUPS ARE NOT

- They are not counseling groups.
- They are not places to "fix" or change women.
- They are not Bible study or prayer groups as such, although Scripture and prayer are a natural framework for the meetings.
- They are not places where women concentrate on themselves and "stay there." Instead they provide opportunity to grow in self-responsibility and wholeness in Christ.

Small groups often rotate leadership among participants, but because support groups usually meet for a specific time period with a specific mutual issue, it works well for a team of coleaders to be responsible for the

Support Groups—Places of Growth and Healing

meetings. As you can see, leadership is important! Let's take a look at it.

WHAT ARE THE PERSONAL LEADERSHIP QUALIFICATIONS OF A SUPPORT GROUP LEADER?

Courage (1 Cor. 16:13, 14)

A leader shows courage in the following ways as a willingness to:

- She must be open to self-disclosure, admitting her own mistakes and taking the same risks she expects others to take.
- She should lovingly explore areas of struggle with women, and look beyond their behavior to hear what's in their hearts.
- The leader is secure in her own beliefs, sensitive to the Holy Spirit's promptings, and willing to act upon them.
- The leader draws on her own experiences to help her identify with others in the group and be emotionally touched by them.
- She continually examines her own life in the light of God's Word and the Holy Spirit's promptings.
- The leader is direct and honest with members, not using her role to protect herself from interaction with the group.
- A group leader knows that wholeness is the goal and that change is a process.

Willingness to Model (Ps. 139:23, 24)

- A group leader should have had some moderate victory in her own struggles, with adequate healing having taken place. If she is not whole in the area she is leading, she should at least be fully aware of her unhealed areas

Sock Hunting and Other Pursuits

and not be defensive of them. She should be open to those who can show her if she is misguiding others by ministering out of her own hurt.

• She understands that group leaders lead largely by example, by doing what she expects members to do.

• She is no longer "at war" with her past and can be compassionate to those who may have victimized her. Yet she is a "warrior woman," strong in her resistance of Satan with a desire to see other captives set free.

Presence (Gal. 6:2)

• A group leader needs to either have had personal experience with a support group, or observed enough so she understands how they function.

• A group leader needs to be emotionally present with the group members, being touched by others' pain, struggles, and joys.

• She needs to be in touch with her own feelings so that she can have compassion for and empathy with the other women.

• She must understand that her role is as a facilitator. She is not to be the answer person nor is she responsible for change in others. Yet she must be able to evidence leadership qualities that enable her to gather a group around her.

Goodwill and Caring (Matt. 22:27, 28)

• A group leader needs to express genuine caring, even for those who are not easy to care for. That takes a commitment to love and a sensitivity to the Holy Spirit.

• She should be able to express caring by: (1) inviting women to participate but allowing them to decide how far to go; (2) giving warmth, concern, and support when, and only when, it is genuinely felt; (3) gently confronting a participant when there are obvious discrepancies between

Support Groups—Places of Growth and Healing

her words and her behavior; and (4) encouraging people to be who they are without their masks and shields.
- She will need to be able to maintain focus in the group.

Openness (Eph. 4:15, 16)
- A group leader must be aware of herself, open to others in the group, open to new experiences, and open to life-styles and values that are different from her own.
- As the leader she needs to have an *attitude* of openness, not revealing every aspect of her personal life, but disclosing enough of herself to give participants a sense of who she is.
- A group leader needs to recognize her own weaknesses and not spend energy concealing them from others. A strong sense of awareness allows her to be vulnerable with the group.

Nondefensiveness (1 Pet. 5:5)
- A group leader needs to be secure in her leadership role. When negative feelings are expressed she must be able to explore them in a nondefensive manner.

Stamina (Eph. 6:10)
- A group leader needs physical and emotional stamina and the ability to withstand pressure and remain vitalized until the group sessions end.
- She must be aware of her own energy level, have outside sources of spiritual and emotional nourishment, and have realistic expectations for the group's progress.

Perspective (Prov. 3:5, 6)
- A group leader needs to cultivate a healthy perspective which allows her to enjoy humor and be comfortable with the release of it at appropriate times in a meeting.

Sock Hunting and Other Pursuits

- Although she will hear pain and suffering, she must trust the Lord to do the work and not take responsibility for what he alone can do.
- She needs to have a good sense of our human condition and God's love, as well as a good sense of timing that allows her to trust the Holy Spirit to work in the women's lives.

Creativity (Phil. 1:9-11)
- She needs to be flexible and spontaneous, able to discover fresh ways to approach each session.

WHAT SPECIFIC SKILLS DOES A LEADER NEED?

A support group leader needs to be competent and comfortable with basic group communications skills. The following five are essential for healthy and open interaction:

Rephrase
- Paraphrase back to the speaker what you thought she said. Example: "I hear you saying that you felt . . ."

Clarify
- To make sure you heard correctly ask the speaker to explain further. Example: "I'm not hearing exactly what you meant when you said . . ."

Extend
- Encourage the speaker to be more specific. Example: "Can you give us an example . . ."

Ask for Input
- Give the other women opportunity to share their opinions. Example: "Does anyone else have any insight on this?"

Support Groups—Places of Growth and Healing

Be Personal and Specific
- Use women's names and convey "I" messages instead of "you" messages. "I'm feeling afraid of your reaction," instead of "You scare me."

ADDITIONAL COMMUNICATION SKILLS

Active Listening
- A good listener learns to "hear" more than the words that are spoken. She absorbs the content, notes the gestures, the body language, the subtle changes in voice or expression, and senses the unspoken underlying messages.
- As a good listener, a leader will need to discern those in the group who need professional counseling and be willing to address this.

Empathy
- This requires sensing the subjective world of the participant—and caring. Of grasping another's experience and at the same time listening objectively.

Respect and Positive Regard
- In giving support, leaders need to draw on the positive assets of the members. Where differences occur, there needs to be open and honest appreciation and acceptance.
- Leaders must be able to maintain confidentiality and instill that emphasis in the group.

Expressing Warmth
- Smiling is especially important in communicating warmth to a group. Other nonverbal expressions are: voice tone, posture, body language, and facial expression.

Genuineness
- Leaders need to be real, to be themselves in relating

Sock Hunting and Other Pursuits

with others, to be authentic and spontaneous, to realize that the Holy Spirit works naturally.

WHAT DOES A LEADER ACTUALLY DO?

The leader will need to establish the atmosphere of the support group and show by her style how to relate lovingly and helpfully in the group. She needs to have God's heart for God's people. The following outline specific tasks.

She Organizes Logistics
- The leader helps arrange initial details of the early meetings—time, place, books, etc. (Note: Leaders need to be aware that much secular material, though good in information, is humanistic in application. "I" and "Self" are the primary focus, rather than Christ.)

She Provides Sense of Purpose and Vision
- She reminds the group of their purpose from time to time so that the group remains focused.

She Acts as the Initiator
- She makes sure everyone knows each other, helps them get acquainted and feel comfortable with each other. Makes sure meetings start and end on time.

She Continues as an Encourager to Group Members
- This means basically: encouraging feelings to be expressed, keeping the atmosphere nonjudgmental and accepting, giving feedback, answering questions, clarifying things that were expressed, etc. Praying with and for members.

She Sets Expectations
- She models openness and interest in the group. She

Support Groups—Places of Growth and Healing

must be willing to take risks by resolving conflicts and clarifying intentions. She holds up standards of confidentiality personally and by reminding the group at each meeting. Confidentiality is crucial to the health of a group, and women should not divulge any private sharing, even to spouses, family, etc.

• She must be watchful and able to guide individuals away from destructive responses. Example: "I have a right to be hurt." She will need to always separate the person from her behavior, meeting the person where she is. Example: "We accept that you are hurt. Do you need to talk about it?"

She Is Sensitive to the Spirit

• She must know when someone needs to be referred to a professional counselor, pastor, etc. and be willing to work that problem through.

• She should be comfortable in ministering freely in the gifts of the Holy Spirit.

She Gives the Guidelines

• It is important that the women know the "ground rules." The leader needs to repeat these often, and *always* when newcomers attend. The following are basic support group guidelines:

1. You have come to give and receive support. No "fixing." We are to listen, support, and be supported by one another, not give advice.

2. Let other members talk. Please let them finish without interruption.

3. Try to step over any fear of sharing in the group. Yet do not monopolize the group's time.

4. Be interested in what someone else shares. Listen with your heart. Never converse privately with someone

Sock Hunting and Other Pursuits

while another woman is talking or belittle her beliefs or expressions.

5. Be committed to express your feelings from the heart. Encourage others to do the same. It's all right to feel angry, to laugh, or to cry.

6. Help others own their feelings and take responsibility for change in their lives. Don't jump in with an easy answer or a story on how you conquered their problem or automatically give scripture as a "pat answer." Relate to where they are.

7. Avoid accusing or blaming. Speak in the "I" mode about how something or someone made you feel. Example: "I felt angry when. . . ."

8. Avoid ill-timed humor to lighten emotionally charged times. Let participants work through their sharing even if it is hard.

9. Keep names and sharing of other group members confidential.

10. Because we are all in various stages of growth, please give others permission to be where they are in their growth. This is a "safe place" for all to grow and share their lives.

She Handles Group Discussion

Everyone is different. Your support group will have a variety of personalities. As a leader you will need to protect the group from problem behavior and help the individuals work through it. The following are examples of ways to help each person contribute so that the group benefits:

THEIR BEHAVIOR	YOUR ACTION
Too talkative	Interject by summarizing what the talker is saying. Turn to someone else in the group and redirect a

	question. "Elaine, what do you feel about that?"
A "fixer"	Show appreciation for their help and insight. Then direct a question to someone else. It is important to draw others in so that the woman needing help gets a healthy perspective on her situation and doesn't close off with a quickie solution.
Rambler	Thank them. If necessary, even break in, comment briefly, and move the discussion on.
Antagonist	Recognize legitimate objections when you can. Turn their comments to a constructive view. If all else fails, discuss the attitude privately and ask for their help.
Obstinate	Ask them to clarify. They may honestly not understand what you're talking about. Enlist others to help them see the point. If that doesn't work, tell them you will discuss the matter after the meeting.
Wrong topic	Focus on the subject. Say something like: "Mary, that's interesting, but tonight we're talking about...."

Sock Hunting and Other Pursuits

Her own problems	Bring it into the discussion if it is related. Otherwise, acknowledge the problem and say: "Yes, I can see why that hurts you. Could we talk about it privately?"
Controversial questions	State clearly what you can or cannot discuss. Say something like: "Problems do exist, but we do not discuss political issues here."
Side conversations	Stop and draw them into your discussion by asking for their ideas.
Personality clash	If a dispute erupts, cut across with a direct question on the topic. Bring others into the discussion: "Let's concentrate on the issue and not make this a personal thing."
Wrong choice of words	Point out that their idea is good and then help them by putting their idea into your words. Protect them from ridicule.
Definitely wrong	Make a clear comment, in an affirming way. "That's another point of view and of course you're entitled to your opinion." Then move on.

Support Groups—Places of Growth and Healing

Bored	Try to find where their area of interest is. Draw them in to share their experience.
Question you can't answer	Redirect the question to the group. If you don't know the answer, say so and offer to find out.
Never participates	Use direct questions. Remind the group that they will get more out of the meeting when they open up.
Quiet, unsure of self	Affirm them in the eyes of the group. Ask direct questions you are sure they can answer.

She Evaluates the Meeting

• Support groups are a growing experience for everyone, including the leader. Don't be afraid to deal with habitual problems.

• Periodically involve the total group in evaluating how things are going.

She Understands Conflict and Can Handle it Positively

• She understands the biblical pattern for making peace with our sisters in Christ. (See Matthew 5:9 and Romans 14:19.)

• She understands that Jesus has given us clear guidelines to resolve conflict and effect reconciliation and that our motive must be to demonstrate God's love, not vengeance. (See Matthew 5:23, 24 and Matthew 18:15-17.)

• She understands that we approach all situations humbly, knowing that none of us is without sin (Gal. 6:1-4)

Sock Hunting and Other Pursuits

and that we are seeking reconciliation and forgiveness, not proving who is right and who is wrong.
- She avoids sermonizing.
- She knows that every group will experience conflict on their way to becoming mature and effective, but uses it to help clarify goals and boundaries for the group.
- She defines and describes the conflict as "our group problem."
- She deals with issues rather than personalities.
- She takes one issue at a time.
- She tries to catch issues while they are small rather than letting them escalate over time.
- She invites cooperation, rather than intimidating or giving ultimatums.
- She expresses need for full disclosure of all the facts rather than allowing hidden agendas or leftover hurt feelings.
- She tries to maintain a friendly, trusting attitude.
- She recognizes others' feelings and concerns and opts for a "win-win" feeling or an "us and them" attitude.
- She encourages the expression of as many new ideas and as much new information as possible to broaden the perspective of all involved.
- She involves every woman in the conflict at a common meeting.
- She clarifies whether she is dealing with one conflict or several on-going ones.

She Knows How to Use Feedback
- Feedback helps another person get information on her behavior.
- Feedback is essential in a support group to help the women keep on target and more effectively move through her problems.

Support Groups—Places of Growth and Healing

- She helps make feedback specific. Example: "Just now when we were talking about forgiveness, you changed the subject and started to blame your brother."
- She directs feedback toward behavior that the receiver can do something about. Example: "Would you like to make a choice to release your judgment against your friend?"
- She takes into account the needs of both the receiver and the giver of feedback. It can be destructive if it's given to "straighten out" someone, rather than lovingly point out where that person is.
- She knows feedback is most useful when it is asked for. She can say: "Margaret, are you open to some feedback?"
- She watches for good timing. She tries to give feedback at the earliest opportunity after the given behavior occurs.
- She checks to ensure clear communication. One way of doing this is to have the receiver paraphrase the feedback to see if that is what the sender meant. Example: "I heard you saying that I need to examine my motives for. . . ."

ONE FINAL WORD

Be encouraged, if the Lord has called you to be a support group leader or a member of a group. The Lord promises to do the work of healing, to be with us, to grant us patience, love, mercy—everything we need to follow his commission to love. There will be hard and even painful times. But we can count on him. "He who began a good work in you (in us) will carry it on to completion until the day of Christ Jesus" (Phil. 1:6).